Effective
Communication
For
Today's Manager

Effective Communication For Today's Manager

James G. Robbins
Barbara S. Jones

Lebhar-Friedman Books
CHAIN STORE PUBLISHING CORP.
A Subsidiary of Lebhar-Friedman, Inc., New York

Prepared for

Cornell University Home Study Program
Department of Agricultural Economics
New York State College of Agriculture and Life Sciences
A Statutory College of the State University

The Advisory Board for the Cornell University Home Study Program has
reviewed this book and recommends it for use by members of the food
industry.

It is the policy of Cornell University actively to support equality of educational and employment opportunity. No person shall be denied admission
to any educational program or activity or be denied employment on the
basis of any legally prohibited discrimination involving, but not limited to,
such factors as race, color, creed, religion, national or ethnic origin, sex,
age, or handicap. The University is committed to the maintenance of affirmative action programs which will assure the continuation of such
equality of opportunity.

Printed in the United States of America
Library of Congress Catalog Card Number: 85-73589
International Standard Book Number: 0-86730-574-6

Contents

Contents

Introduction

As you begin to read this book, stop for a moment and think about your day on the job. Try to remember each problem, task, conversation, and interview as well as the entire scope and variety of things you had to do. Don't forget the phone calls and the talks with salespeople, or the group from the Jaycees who wanted you to provide space for a booth for one of their projects.

Then recall the time spent on your monthly report and the letter of recommendation you wrote for one of your former employees. How about the long memo from the district manager outlining some upcoming changes in operational procedures? (You made a mental note to call a meeting to prepare your staff for those changes.) Next, you took some time to scan the newspaper to check what other businesses were doing.

In your review of activities, don't forget the weekly meeting of your civic club where you listened to a speech by one of the city "fathers" who was talking about some long-range goals of the community. (You remember thinking that the speaker made some points, but, all in all, his long-winded approach would cure anyone's insomnia.) Oh yes, and when you returned from the meeting you learned that one of the cashiers had to leave because of illness, and you spent 20 minutes trying to find someone who could come in for the rest of the day. And so it went.

Of course, that was part of a purely hypothetical day. You probably didn't have all these problems, and you undoubtedly had others that were not mentioned. But the point is that you spent most of your time involved in some kind of communication activity. That hardly should come as a surprise to you, but now that you look back over the list, it may surprise you to see that almost everything you did can be called a communication. Research tells us that the average manager spends between 70 and 80 percent of his or her time in one form or another of communication: talking, listening, reading, or writing.

Let's review the role of a manager. What are the dimensions of the job? It is obvious that to have an organization, there must be a goal or purpose for its being. In your case, as with many organizations, the goal is to make a profit. If you cannot do that, you will not survive.

Perhaps the most important dimension of any organization is its people. At times you may wish you could eliminate them, but if you did, there would be no reason for your job, which is really one of communicating with and managing people.

A business's goal cannot be achieved without its people, nor does a business exist under circumstances where one person is acting alone. Simply stated, your job is to make a profit, and you do this through the utilization and cooperation of many people. You are actually in the people business. In a real sense you are more a manager of people than of a business.

Your concern for people should not be limited to those you "manage," however; it also includes those you serve—the customers. As you well know, your customers judge your whole organization by the positive or negative behavior (particularly the communication) of one employee.

What is the role of communication in your particular job? All organizations, no matter what their size or scope, are held together by and perform their functions through the process of communication. Communication is the channel of influence, the mechanism of change, the means of motivation, and the socializing agent which enables an organization to reach its goal. Without communication there can be no interpersonal interaction, no groups, no government, not even a society as we know it today. Chaos would reign.

Communication is a central part of everything we do. Most "people" problems can be traced in part or in full to poor communication, a breakdown in communication, or no communication at all. Human interaction succeeds or fails as a direct function of our ability to communicate.

There is no such thing as a special kind of communication for managers, or for druggists, or teachers, or lawyers, or for any specific group of business or professional people. Each organization has its special communication problems and barriers. This book attempts to deal with and apply the theory and technique of human communication to the special needs and problems of a manager.

We have tried to select the areas of chief concern in the communication life of a manager, assistant manager, or prospective manager. In order to understand better what the communication problems are, we spent many hours in businesses as customers, observers, and interviewers. We asked managers and employees what aspects of their work were rewarding, puzzling, or frustrating. We asked for suggestions on how procedures and policies could be improved. For their frank appraisals and willingness to let us follow them around asking questions, we are indebted to a great many people.

In Chapter One, we start with the "Big Picture," an overview of communication as a process, loaded with misconceptions as well as conceptions. In Chapter Two we focus on the *person* involved in interpersonal communication, and how "who" we think we are—our self-concept—plays a vital role. Messages and meanings are the subjects of Chapter Three in which we take a look at such concepts as content and intent, fact and inference, and the differences between them.

A relatively new aspect of communication theory—nonverbal communication—is the subject of Chapter Four. This is where we examine, among other things, the influence of how we look and sound in relation to what we say.

Feedback is a very common term today. In Chapter Five, we analyze what feedback really is, the various types of feedback response, and ways to elicit helpful feedback, a vital ingredient in any successful communication. Sharpening the specific skills of communication is the subject of Chapter Six.

The first six chapters deal primarily with interpersonal, one-to-one communication. Chapter Seven discusses concepts and problems involved in interviewing; the focus broadens out from one-to-one communication to one-to-a-few and one-to-many. With Chapters Seven and Eight, we begin to look at group communication, starting with interviewing. It may come as a surprise how much interviewing managers actually do and how they can unexpectedly become interviewees instead of interviewers.

With meetings taking up so much of a manager's time, Chapter Eight points out potential pitfalls and suggestions for improvement for both group leaders and participants. Chapter Nine covers two keys to effective management—decision-making and problem-solving—both of which may be handled on an individual basis but are more often tackled by groups.

The final chapter deals with communicating up, down, and across an organizational network. Each of us is only a crossroads in a larger pattern of interconnecting pathways where messages are going in all directions. We need to understand how these paths work as well as the messages that are constantly traveling back and forth.

If it were possible, we would like to thank all the people whose ideas have influenced ours and all those who have encouraged us to express our own. Perhaps the publication of this book will, in itself, be an expression of both our debt and our gratitude.

JAMES GAMBRELL ROBBINS
BARBARA SCHINDLER JONES

1
The Big Picture— Communicatively Speaking

What Communication Is All About

As a manager, you are well aware that much research and money have gone into the art and science of effective packaging. A package attracts, reminds, informs, and sells. The customer selects the package desired and pays for it, completing the transaction. The product prepared is the product received. There is little loss or change in the transfer.

But what happens when we try to package and deliver an idea? Transferring information, thoughts, and feelings is not so simple. Rather than being a product, communication is a process. Rather than being a specific item which can be handed from one person to another, communication is a dynamic, flowing, ever-changing phenomenon. Because of its quicksilver, fluid nature, communication is hard to nail down. It's something like trying to understand

1

what a river is like by dipping out a bucket of water and looking at it. In order to study communication, we must stop the very process that is its essence.

When we speak, we do not wrap up our meanings in word packages and deliver them to our listener. There is no way to "hand over" an idea to someone else. When we communicate, the best we can do is try to awaken, through verbal and visual symbols, meanings and experiences that the listener already has acquired. Only these sounds and signs can be sent out; and because everyone has a different storehouse of signs and sounds, we know immediately that no two people can ever share exactly the same meanings. Therefore, what one person sends out as a communication may be slightly different or even greatly distorted by another person's receiving act.

Misconceptions About Communication

1. "What's so hard about communication? Everybody does it." One of the most damaging misconceptions about communication is the illusion of it. It appears easy, and it's true that everyone does it. We've communicated all our lives, and it's just as natural as breathing. Why the big fuss?

Just because something appears to be natural doesn't mean we are necessarily good at it. (Most people could even improve their methods of breathing!) Communication is so commonplace that we tend to overlook its complexity and would just as soon not be reminded that we lack competence in our most basic and personal activity. Especially if it's true.

However, if we are to become more successful communicators, we will get further faster if we start with an awareness that, although communicating seems easy, communicating effectively is one of the most difficult and complex acts we will ever have to perform.

2. "Everybody knows what communication is." We glibly use the term "communication" without being aware that it is one of the most misunderstood yet overworked words we have. We use it without any general agreement as to its meaning. For example, a recent study found more than *2,600 different definitions* for the term. The word has been used to describe everything from a party invitation to the Ten Commandments.

What does the word mean to you? Is it communication when a customer frowns at your "Good morning"? You bet it is! Although it may have been an unintentional message, it's still a message. Communication means much more than the simple flow of information. It is concerned with emotions, attitudes, morals, motivation, climate, physical setting, the situation, and more—it is concerned with people and their egos.

If we consider thinking as the foundation of communication (because every purposeful communication begins with a thought or idea), we can build two wings on the foundation. One we will call "Transmitting Skills"—speaking and writing; the other we will identify as "Receiving Skills" which includes listening and reading. A skill which has only recently come to be recognized as important to both transmitting and receiving is nonverbal communication—messages that are separate from words or go along to supplement words. (See Figure 1.) We will come back to these skills in a later chapter, but we must not forget that they are all encompassed by the word "communication."

3. "I have spoken; therefore I have communicated." As David Berlo points out in his book, *The Process of Communication*, whenever you hear someone say, "I TOLD THEM" ("and they didn't do it," or "they were too stupid to get it"), you know that person believes that meanings are in words and that all he or she has to do is find the right words.[1] Words don't "mean"; people "mean." More about this, too, in a later chapter.

Figure 1 Principal Communication Skills

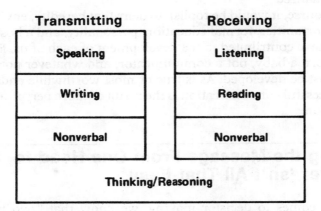

1. David Berlo, *The Process of Communication* (New York: Holt, Rinehart, and Winston, 1960), p. 177.

4. "Communication happens only when I want it to." Have you ever watched a speaker who was obviously nervous and uptight walk to the podium? You can almost hear his knees rattle; his shoulders droop as he shuffles along hesitantly. Then he makes a valiant effort to overcome his stage fright by squaring his shoulders, looking the audience in its collective eye, and speaking in clear, positive tones. Such a person believes that he hasn't begun to communicate until he opens his mouth and words come out. He isn't aware that his nonverbal messages of nervousness and insecurity have been so loud and clear that his verbal messages are likely to be lost.

We all communicate all of the time. There is no way to stop the process. It doesn't just happen when we want it to. Even when we are alone we communicate with ourselves. Awake, we call it thinking or daydreaming; asleep, we call it dreaming.

5. "Communicators are born, not made—some have it and some don't." This one is a real stopper. If you believe this, there is little chance that you will improve or change—or that you will even finish reading this book! Communication is learned behavior, and therefore it can be changed and improved.

The ability to be an effective communicator is not a divine gift reserved for a select few. Effective communication is an achievement, not a birthright or happy accident of heredity. Everyone has the potential for effective communication, and this potential can be more fully actualized.

Of course, it would be foolish to deny that heredity, environment, past opportunities, formal education, personality, and a host of other factors have contributed to the development of each of us. But everyone is born a baby, not a communicator, and whatever potential we have must be developed. As is true of most worthwhile endeavors in life, successful communication is the result of more perspiration than inspiration.

Getting the Message From One Head to Another Isn't All That Easy

When it comes to decision-making, we know that "two heads are better than one." The knowledge and experience contained in two minds are bound to be broader than that contained in one mind. This factor is a definite plus when a group is trying to solve a problem or make the best possible decision. However, this same factor is what gets us into trouble in interpersonal communication.

No two people—not even identical twins—have had exactly the same background and experience; therefore, no two people can have identical meanings for anything. Moreover, each individual has a unique picture of who he or she is. This picture, this idea of who we think we are, is called the "self-concept." It is private and personal, and it may or may not resemble what other people would call "reality." One person's self-concept is positive; another's is negative. Also, someone might see himself only in terms of the self he would like to be—the self he is striving to become.

It is with this unique self-concept, whatever shape it takes, that each person's communication begins. If you hope to communicate with another person, you would do well to try to understand his idea of who he is—his own self-concept. And this may be a country-mile away from your idea of who he is.

One way to look at communication between two people is the idea that Rudolph Flesch had in mind when, years ago, he described Mr. A. and Mr. B. standing on two sides of a chasm.[2] The chasm is too deep and too wide to jump across, and it is certainly impossible for Mr. A. and Mr. B. to reach across.

The only way that Mr. A. can get a message to Mr. B. across this chasm is for Mr. A. to say or do something that will stimulate Mr. B. to want to help build a bridge. If each man helps construct what Flesch calls an "emotional bridge," they can communicate. Neither man can do it by himself. One of the best things that Mr. A. can do is to show Mr. B. why he should help build the bridge; Mr. A.'s message should make it very clear what's in it for Mr. B. If Mr. A. does not communicate Mr. B.'s stake in the transaction, Mr. A. is only talking to himself.

The Communication Process

With this background we can now look more closely at the ingredients which make up the communication process. Suppose you are a manager. Walking through your place of business, you notice that something has fallen on the floor and has broken. You find one of your employees and say, "Walt, will you stop what you're doing and clean

---

2. Rudolph Flesch, *How to Make Sense* (New York: Harper and Brothers, 1954), p. 182.

up the mess over there, please?" Walt responds, "Yes, sir. I'll get right on it." You go on about your affairs, but you notice that Walt is, in fact, cleaning the area as you requested.

What happened in this simple communication incident? You were the *source*, or the beginning, of the communication process. You felt a need to communicate, and to do this, you had to put your needs into understandable symbols or words. This is the process of *encoding:* the selection of signals which can convey your message to Walt. Then you *transmitted* the signals through the air waves which were your *medium* or *channel.* (If you had written Walt a note, paper and pencil would have been your medium.) This procedure represents only half of the process, the transmitting.

Next comes the receiving part. Walt heard the signals and properly *decoded* them into thoughts which were meaningful to him. The process of decoding is obviously the reverse of the encoding that you performed. Walt was the destination of your message, and since both of you shared a common field of experience, communication was possible. The greater the similarity of your fields of experience, the more likely it will be that the message received is understood in the way that the message-sender had in mind.

Communication has a *purpose.* We communicate because we want someone to act, think, or feel in a certain way; we know we have communicated when our desired response is achieved. In this case, Walt quickly cleaned up the mess and, by both his words and his actions, gave you *feedback* that he had understood the message and its purpose.

By way of reviewing this simple communication act as an example of the process, we can list the following communication ingredients:

1. There must be a sender, who is the source of the message.
2. Each communication must have a purpose.
3. The idea is encoded into symbols or signals.
4. The symbols or signals are transmitted through a channel.
5. The receiver decodes the symbols or signals by giving them meaning.
6. If the sender and receiver share some degree of common experience, the chances are better that they will also share the sender's intended meaning.
7. Feedback is what happens as a result of the communication and is the primary way we have of checking to see if the message has been understood.

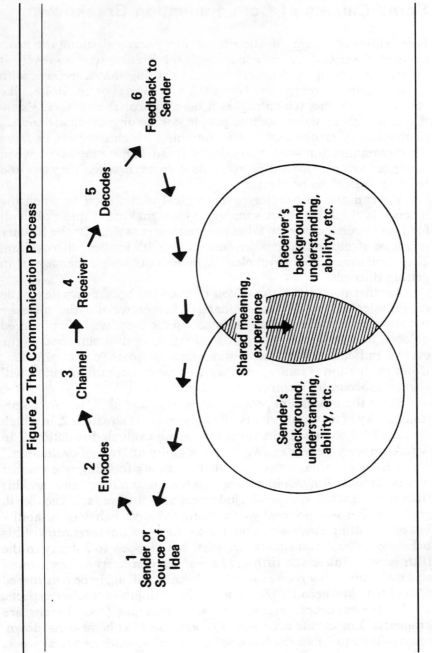

Figure 2 The Communication Process

1 Sender or Source of Idea

2 Encodes

3 Channel

4 Receiver

5 Decodes

6 Feedback to Sender

Sender's background, understanding, ability, etc.

Shared meaning, experience

Receiver's background, understanding, ability, etc.

Some Causes of Communication Breakdown

Possibilities of communication breakdown occur all along the process just described. A principal cause of breakdown, however, is "noise," which in this context means anything that interferes with transmission or reception. We can encounter channel noise, like static on the radio, which makes it hard to hear the speaker. Extraneous sounds or sights, such as people talking or moving around us, or machinery clanks and whirs—anything which distracts us from the communication—are examples of noise. Noise may occur when messages are overloaded or redundant or even when they are too brief or sketchy to be clear.

We can also encounter psychological noise, such as when the listener is thinking about something else, making it quite difficult for him to concentrate on what the speaker is saying. Or the listener might be afraid of the speaker, be at odds with him, or distrust him. These and many other psychological factors can keep a message from getting through.

Another potential cause of communication breakdown lies in the communicators' ability to evaluate. Whether we are the message sender or receiver, it is up to us to size up the event we have observed or been told about and evaluate it along several dimensions. Is the event significant? Should we communicate about it? To whom? When? If our evaluation is faulty, chances are that our communication will also be inaccurate, incomplete, or irrelevant.

Since the evaluation process takes time and skill, we are sometimes guilty of taking shortcuts. We may evaluate situation 2, in which we now find ourselves, the same way as we evaluated situation 1, in which we were yesterday. We are then guilty of "frozen evaluation."

A frozen evaluation occurs when Johnny's fourth grade teacher writes "Johnny is a troublemaker" on his cumulative record, and his fifth grade teacher accepts the judgment as if it were fact. The fourth grade teacher was not really describing Johnny's behavior or ability but only putting down a personal assessment or interpretation of his behavior. Would you like to bet what will happen to Johnny in the fifth grade? Unless the fifth grade teacher can keep an open mind and make his or her own evaluation, Johnny will again be considered a troublemaker because that is what the fifth grade teacher expects.

Whenever people are viewed as stereotypes ("All Texans are braggarts") or events are seen as repetitions ("This business downtown will be just like the last one"), frozen evaluations are at work.

It is not only difficult, it is impossible to evaluate each event or person without being influenced by past encounters. However, successful communicators do their best to be objective and to look for what is special or unique about a particular person or a particular event. They constantly strive for a fresh appraisal and try to leave the frozen or canned evaluations on the shelf.

2
Person-to-Person Communication

How do managers manage?

This question can be answered in many ways; it largely depends upon whom you ask. One thing is sure, however; and that is whoever a manager is or whatever managerial style he follows, his work is never cut-and-dried and never an impersonal process.

ROI is an acronym readily recognized by managers as meaning "Return On Investment." This is, naturally, a vital concern of any business. But ROI can also mean "Return On Individuals." Managers manage people; it is through these people that a business succeeds or fails. A manager's primary responsibility is the development of a team which works with him rather than for him. If he can accomplish this, the likelihood of realizing the maximum return from individuals and achieving the goals of the organization is greatly enhanced.

Management can be regarded as the art of relating to people, and it will remain an art rather than a science as long as peoples' attitudes, intelligence, feelings, and reactions cannot be programmed like a computer or directed by rote. But just as any artist uses tools to accomplish his art so must a manager use all of the tools at his or her disposal. In this chapter we are primarily concerned with the tools that contribute to a better understanding of people.

To work effectively with others one must know something of their personal goals, their needs, their fears and apprehensions. Managerial literature places heavy stress on knowing the other person, and this is certainly important, but we contend that the first step in becoming an effective manager is knowing yourself.

Self-Concept and Communication

All communication begins with the self, and every person sees himself in a very personal and private way. Let's take a closer look at this concept because one's view of self is the most crucial dimension in establishing and maintaining effective communication. Not only is it crucial, but it is also one of the most fragile elements in the communication process. If our self-concept is threatened, our instinctive reaction is to become defensive and protective. When our defenses are marshalled, meaningful communication ceases. "Just who does that guy think he's talking to?" is a typical reaction. Feelings are hurt, effective listening is impossible, and relationships become strained.

Definition of Self-Concept

As human beings, we exist and function on two basic levels: "Who we are" and "Who we think we are." "Who we are" is the real self and includes factual and tangible factors like age, height, weight, education, and marital status. As important as the "real self" is, it does not have the deep significance of the pictures in our heads that represent our ideas of ourselves when relating to, interacting with, or communicating with others. *Who we think we are is much more important than who we are.*

"Who we think we are," or our concept of ourselves, is one of the most controlling factors of our behavior. This is our personal and private sense of identity which, in our eyes, distinguishes us from all others. The development of our self-concept has been going on all our lives, even before we were aware of it. Interaction with others, successful and unsuccessful experiences, evaluations by key individuals in our lives are all vital to the shaping of an awareness of identity. Through this process we seek to answer such questions as: Who am I? How worthy am I? What's unique about me? What do I stand for? What do I believe and value? What are my strengths and weaknesses?

The list of questions is almost limitless and will have a different character for each person. John W. Keltner focuses on some of the qualities of the self and self-concept:

> Self-understanding is the basis for the self-concept. Each of us has certain beliefs about himself. The collection of beliefs about who and what we are goes to make up our self-image or self-concept. *The self-concept is composed of those physical and social perceptions of ourselves that we have acquired through our interaction with others and that have been validated by our experiences.* (author's italics)[1]

During a training program, we asked several managers to write three or more statements that they felt would best describe themselves. They were asked not to identify themselves in any way so that they could be completely honest. They were to state how they really felt and not what they thought would be an appropriate answer. No instructions were given about which area or dimension of their lives they should describe. You will be interested in the following cross-section taken from their actual statements.

Before you look at the list, however, think for a few minutes about how you would describe yourself. Usually when we ask people to do this, they get a very pained look on their faces. It turns out to be difficult—a lot harder than describing someone else. However, if you will put down those attributes that first come to your mind, without cheating by looking ahead to the list, we think you will find it an interesting exercise.

Now let's see how the other managers described themselves. This is only a partial list of what the whole group turned in, but responses have not been edited. These are the actual words used by actual managers.

I am: 5′8″ tall and weigh approximately 168 pounds
       Manager of a division of _____
       A man of 49 years of age, married, and have four children
       Enthusiastic about my work

---

1. John W. Keltner, *Interpersonal Speech-Communication: Elements and Structure* (Belmont, California: Wadsworth Publishing Co., Inc., 1970), p. 45.

Interested in developing better methods and procedures for an improved operation

I am: Interested in people
Trying to be a better human
Curious about life as such

I am: Sales-minded
Aggressive
Community-minded in regard to development and growth
Motivated by profit
Interested in welfare of my employees

I am: Fair and just
Ambitious
Basically lazy
Dependable
Eager to learn more on all subjects

I am: Middle-aged
Fat
Bald
Over-the-hill

I am: Hard working
Lonely
Deserving the best
Self-conscious

I am: Set in my ideas
Not easy to convince
Not a good listener
Particular about the work done by my employees

I am: Sincere in the job that I do
Very careful in the work that I do
Reliable and honest
Trustworthy
Not grouchy or mad-looking when around customers

I am: Hard working
Bad tempered
Good thinker
Financially successful
Extremely hard to please

I am: Moderately energetic, quick in thought and action
Somewhat an individual of moods
Adept at organizing
Fairly pliable

Able to adjust to individual, group, or situation
Inclined to procrastinate
I am: Too outspoken, quick to speak
A talker instead of a listener
A sincere person
A concerned person
A troubled person
I am: A good citizen
A booster of our town
A good family man
I am: Confused by the rapid changes in our business
Frustrated by lack of time to do a job well
A rural type person who got ahead by hard work, not education

You will probably find similarities between the words you selected to describe yourself and some of these statements. When we conduct this self-identity exercise, people almost always are surprised at the similarities ("I didn't know other people felt that way, too.") But what is even more surprising to most people, considering that the group has the same profession in common, is how varied the list is. There are always a wide range of concepts and a great variety of ways to express these intimate attributes.

So far, we have talked about the self-concept as an entity. Now, let's look at some of its facets. We have a concept about our physical self, our intellectual self, our social self, our psychological self, and our ideal self. You will see all of these facets reflected in the list of statements.

The Physical Self-Concept

The way we look is extremely important to us. Note that in the first statement from the managers, one said he was 5 feet, 8 inches tall and weighed approximately 168 pounds. Since he listed these factors first, it is a fairly safe assumption that he sees himself in physical terms.

But how we see ourselves, even physically, may not be very objective. Don't we put on our "best face" when we catch a glimpse of ourselves frowning in a mirror; don't we suck in our abdomens to look just a little slimmer?

In one interview with an assistant manager, he said, "I've gone about as far as I can go in this job." He was a young man, and we were understandably curious as to why he would make such a statement. Since he seemed willing to discuss the matter, we asked him to explain. "Well, all you have to do is look at me!" he exclaimed. "I don't *look* like a manager. I'm short, too plain—just mousey looking. They'll never make a manager out of me."

In our judgment, he had made a very unrealistic and harsh assessment of his own physical appearance. However, the point here is not the possession of certain physical traits that are important, but rather how an individual feels about them. It is what he thinks he is that governs his behavior. In our culture we are continually reminded how wonderful it is to be tall, dark, and handsome. The "Man of Distinction," the "Best Dressed Woman," and all the "Beautiful People" are constantly projected from magazines and television screens. Few of us can measure up to these images. The person who can look himself or herself in the mirror, realistically, but not overcritically, and say, "Okay, I am what I am so I'll make the most of what I have," has a much better physical self-concept than the manager who was convinced that the shape of his body would prevent his future success.

The Intellectual Self-Concept

We live in a society in which education and knowledge are often synonymous with power and prestige. Let's return to some of the statements managers made about themselves—"set in my ideas"; "interested in developing better methods and procedures"; "good thinker"; "quick in thought and action"; "adept at organizing"—such statements indicate that these people see themselves as bright, sharp, firm in ideas, and adept. Again, the point here is not the amount of education or the degree of intellectual acumen we have, but rather how we react to them and apply them.

For example, we know a president of a large bank who did not finish college or get a degree. Although very successful, he is still sensitive about his lack of formal education. We have heard him lament the fact that he did not get a degree. We know him to be a shrewd businessman, both knowledgeable and intelligent, but his concept of his intellectual self is less than he would like it to be.

The Social Self-Concept

We live in a social world. The day of the rugged individual, if it ever really existed, seems to have passed from the scene. Man is, and has always been, a social animal. He must depend upon others for many things, including life itself. The more man lives in himself, the less a whole man he becomes. Therefore, it is no wonder that many of us describe ourselves in social contexts, indicating our relationships with others.

Here are some examples from the original list of responses from managers in our experiment: "Interested in people"; "community-minded in regards to development and growth"; "lonely"; "self-conscious"; "a good citizen"; "a good family man."

Obviously, there is a significant concern about the social self, even in this small sample. Perhaps Alexis de Tocqueville was correct when he observed over a century ago that the American people are the most sociable on earth. Have you noticed that many parents are more concerned with their children being popular than with their education?

We all develop ways of relating to people. We have one way for our family, a way for our customers, one for our superiors, one for our employees, one for our friends, and so on. In each of these groups, we develop networks of relationships with members of that group. The way we view ourselves in our relationships with these other people is an important dimension of the self. All our lives we have been subtly programmed by our relationships with others. Whether we were neglected as a child or whether we had warm, loving relationships with family and friends often adds up to how we see ourselves today as social beings.

The Psychological Self-Concept

Here we are concerned with feelings and attitudes. In addition, the psychological self-concept is also concerned with our attempts to use a facade to cover what we don't like in ourselves or fear others won't like. Another way of looking at it is to think of our private self in contrast with our public self.

Once again let's refer to some of the previous statements which deal with this dimension: "Trying to be a better human"; "deserving the best"; "extremely hard to please"; "a concerned person"; "a troubled person."

By looking back at the whole list you will discover a wide range of concepts from the very positive to the very negative. How honest these descriptions were, we have no way of knowing. Perhaps people were being modest and making use of understatement. It would be of little value to construct lists of desirable or undesirable qualities that all managers should have. There obviously are no right answers.

What is important is some degree of insight into why we act as we do. We may see ourselves in terms of our strengths (pliable, sincere) or weaknesses (an individual of moods, inclined to procrastinate). No one has to tell us that the smart thing to do is to maximize our strengths by making the most of them while, at the same time, admitting our deficiencies and improving them if we can. An inventory of our psychological self-concepts will help us to do just that.

Most management textbooks and authorities contend that the majority of managers who fail do so not because of lack of training, education, or technical or administrative skill, but because of social inadequacies. These inadequacies are not, as a rule, based on the real self but rather on the concept of self. And the interesting part is that as we learn and grow and improve, so do our self-concepts. Both "who we are" and "who we think we are" actually can be changed.

The Ideal Self-Concept

We all have some kind of an idea or image that we would like to become. This is a kind of "the me I must be," or "the me I'd like to be," or "the me I could have been, if only. . . ."

The following statements from the original list suggest possible references to the ideal self-concept or, in some cases, barriers to obtaining such a goal: "Trying to be a better human"; "eager to learn more on all subjects"; "confused by the rapid changes in our business"; "frustrated by lack of time to do a job well."

When we note a discrepancy between our idealized self-concept and our real self, we may either refuse to accept the difference or do everything we can to be like the idealized image. No accuser is more doggedly persistent than one's own conscience or ambition; no judgment is more severe than that passed on oneself by oneself.

We have looked at a variety of ways of describing the self. How do we know which one of these is the real self-concept? (Will the real you please stand up?) They're all real, of course. We are many selves in one. The knowledge of ourselves comes from many places and through many channels and is never complete. But the more we understand ourselves, the better we will relate to and communicate with others. As we expand our understanding of self, we are, at the same time, increasing our potential for effective person-to-person communication.

How Others See You

Without some degree of self-knowledge, it is extremely difficult to understand the dynamic process of interpersonal relationships. The way you see yourself in your own private way is naturally very clear to you. But what do others see? Your employees, friends, and associates may not see the same you that you see. Of course we all have a tendency to see what we expect to see and what we want to see. It's that old dilemma: is believing seeing, or is seeing believing—or both?

In the same training program in which we asked managers to describe themselves, we also asked their subordinates to give us three or more statements which they felt best described the managers. The same instructions were given, with no suggestions about what aspects to select. Because both lists were anonymous we have no way of matching the manager with what his or her subordinates said. Perhaps it's just as well!

He is: Reasonably well educated
Interested in making a good profit
Having an extensive social life
He is: Aggressive to a fault
Mainly concerned about money
Not very cooperative
He is: Neat
Well dressed
Out to get you
She is: Reserved
Shrewd
Honest
Religious
He is: Trying to do the best he can
Keeping a close eye on employees
A show-off

She is: Very neat
Very good in displaying
Very knowledgeable

He is: Much too busy
Not really interested in employees or customers
Passive

He is: Rich
Smart
Aggressive
Independent

He is: Conservative
Able to socially mix with others to advantage
Willing to expound his thinking only to the extent it benefits him

She is: Not aggressive enough
Not progressive
Conservative

He is: Basically dedicated
Not as ambitious as he needs to be
Satisfied
Comfortable

He is: Out for himself
Not too interested in helping a customer
Never able to talk with me

He is: Middle-aged
Middle-class
Middle-of-the road

How do you react to these statements? Do you see a different theme running through the subordinates' list? Although we have not reported all the statements made by either the managers or the subordinates, the following descriptions made by subordinates were never made by the managers about themselves: "extensive social life"; "main concern is money"; "not very cooperative"; "out to get you"; "a show-off"; "not interested in employees or customers"; "out for himself"; "never has time to talk." It is obvious these people really do not know each other, and it is highly likely they are having real difficulty in their person-to-person communication. If management is the art of relating to people, it is clear that more effective tools are needed to accomplish the goal for this group of managers and subordinates.

Bridging the Gap, or Who Am I Really Talking To?

It was near the end of Larry Hines' shift when he received a message to report to the manager's office. Larry had been with the operation for several years and he liked his work, but he was hoping that he could move up to a more responsible position. As he walked toward the office, he wondered what this summons was all about. Carl Palmer, the manager, was new and Larry didn't know him very well. His main impression centered around the fact that one of Carl's first acts had been to trim the staff, "cutting out dead wood," as he described it.

As he entered Carl's office, Larry felt just a bit of apprehension. Carl asked Larry to have a seat, then leaned back in his chair and, for what seemed like a long time to Larry, just looked at him. Finally, Carl said, "I've been watching you pretty closely since I've been here, and I've decided it's time we had a chat about your work and future with us."

Larry's heart sank. Just what he had feared. Then he became angry and blurted out, "So that's why you've been snooping around and taking all those notes. And I guess that's why Joe has been keeping tabs on me, too. Well, let me tell you something, Mr. Big Shot, you can take your job and cram it."

With that, Larry rushed out of the office and slammed the door. Carl tried to stop him, but it was too late. Larry was not only gone from the office; he had left the premises.

Several things went wrong in this person-to-person communication. Carl never did get to inform Larry that he had been selected to attend a management training school and that he was to be promoted to assistant manager after his training. One could argue that with the kind of temper Larry demonstrated, it is just as well that he was gone. But the point of this illustration is that Carl made a very common error. Instead of talking to another person, he was really talking to himself. Carl knew what was in his own head, but he was unaware of the assumptions and perceptions that were in Larry's head. Carl had little, if any, awareness of Larry's world, and therefore communication broke down when Larry's self-concept was threatened. On the other hand, we should not be overly critical of Carl. He probably did what he thought was right and was just as confused as Larry after this encounter.

Just what are the chances that someone can talk to you in terms of *your* you? If you tend to see yourself as you want to be seen by others and this perception of yourself controls your behavior, then the effectiveness of any communication with you depends on how much the other person knows and understands about the way you perceive yourself. In other words, a person must speak to your perception of yourself instead of to his or her perception of you.

But how are we able to do this? The answer can be simply stated, but not as simply done: the better a person knows you and the better you know him or her, the greater are the chances of effective communication. This requires a certain degree of self-disclosure. You must let people see behind facades and public faces; you must allow them to share feelings and work toward a mutual trust. Recall Figure 2 in Chapter One? The goal here is to enlarge the area in which the two circles overlap—to increase shared experiences and meanings.

"Getting to Know You" Isn't as Easy as It Used to Be

People used to work with one another in the knowledge that they probably would be together until retirement. This enhanced the prospect that they would understand each other; trust was a way of life. There was little reason to suspect one another of ulterior motives. But the atmosphere of the business environment has changed drastically. Automation and new technology have resulted in depersonalization, and over-concern with objectivity has tended to thwart old-fashioned caring and intimacy. People change jobs often; they move from city to city without a backward glance. Interpersonal relationships on the job, therefore, have a tentative nature. Managers often don't know their superiors or their employees very well.

Chances are that the instability of relationships is even more prevalent than most people realize. Edward M. Harwell, in his book, *Personnel Management and Training*, reports some relevant data about turnover. In his survey of 5,303 food stores, with 329,395 employees, he found that:

> ... the average eight million dollar supermarket with 63 employees—27 full-timers (43 percent of the staff) and 36 part-timers (57 percent of the staff)—had to hire 28 new employees every year to maintain its normal work force. More than ten

percent of its full-time employees (3), and more than two-thirds of its of part-timers (25), were replaced each year.[2]

What Can a Manager Do?

As a manager, you probably are not too surprised at these figures. But the significance of this situation is the effect it has on establishing effective communication within such a fluid, ever-changing network. What can you, as a manager, do about all this? Although it may sound like an oversimplification, the answer is to *take* the time to know your staff personally and to build an open, two-way rapport in which effective communication is the norm, not the exception. You may argue that you can't afford the time to get to know your people well and to let them know you. But the real question is: can you afford not to?

There are no sure-fire techniques for accomplishing this goal; it is simply not an easily solved problem. You must analyze your own situation with your own employees first. Then, see if the following ideas can help you cope with establishing meaningful relationships and effective communication.

1. How you view the relationship between yourself and an employee determines to a great extent how you will function within it. If you see that relationship as transient, then there is little chance that you will devote time or effort to developing it. But remember that creating the climate in which a relationship can function is primarily the manager's responsibility. It would be very unusual if a young part-timer took the initiative to establish an open and sharing relationship. Harwell points out that many food store employees start as part-time workers. It is, therefore, essential that a meaningful relationship be established at the outset—a relationship that can only be initiated by you, the manager.

2. If you are to establish an effective relationship, you should avoid the tendency to communicate from the base of your title, position, or status. You probably have noticed how close the word "communication" is to the words common, community, and communion. It is what you have in common with the other person that

2. Edward M. Harwell, *Personnel Management and Training* (New York: Chain Store Publishing Corp., 1987), p. 2.

determines the limits within which communication can occur. If there is little in common, there usually is little communication.

"Community" refers to shared objectives, values, attitudes, and interests. Without a sense of community, attempts to establish interaction are fruitless. This is as true of relationships between people as it is between nations. How destructive it is when managers, under the mistaken notion that they cannot otherwise be impartial or fair, seek to increase psychological distance between themselves and their employees and customers. If we "commune," we seek to be as open and authentic as the situation requires.

We also need to show other people the courtesy of listening—really listening—to what they have to say, even though they may disagree or find fault with us.

When you can do these things, you are making progress in understanding the other person's world. Remember that other people are at the center of their own world of psychological experience. The real for them is the reality they experience, not what you tell them.

3. When trying to understand the self-concept of another person, try to adopt his or her frame of reference and be mindful of the other viewpoint. This means more than putting yourself in the other person's shoes; it is more like getting into his skin, thinking his thoughts, seeing his world, feeling his feelings. Thinking and feeling for and about the other person is desirable, but thinking and feeling with him is far more productive. There is a great risk that you will disagree with what you see and hear through such a process. But the purpose of getting out of one's self and into the other is for understanding, not necessarily agreement. Once you have developed insight into how the other person views reality, how he sees himself, and how he values your mutual relationship, you will be able to fashion your communication so that it will be truly effective. And you will avoid the trap of talking to yourself.

One last point. As a manager, your goal is to communicate, not to impress. Effective communication is not a battle of wits nor a semantic handball game. Through communication, you are seeking to develop a team that will achieve mutual goals. The sender of communication is more the servant than the master of the communication receiver. It is true that the listener controls the speaker. If the speaker feels listeners are inattentive or in disagreement, the speaker has the burden of shifting the message. The listener or reader decides if he or she wants to hear or read.

You may be able to dictate the manner of communication, but you have no way of commanding a certain response. You have the task of building that emotional bridge referred to before. Moreover, you must inspire the receiver of your message to want to build his or her half of the bridge.

3
Messages and Meanings

One day you walk into the back room and find two employees in a heated argument, almost ready to come to blows. Just as you arrive, you hear one shout, "I don't care what you *meant*, I heard what you *said!*" You are able to calm them down, but, as you return to your office, you remember what you heard. What did that mean? Are words more important than what we "mean" by them? Wouldn't that argument have been avoided if the employee had a better vocabulary and had therefore been better able to say what he meant? How does one find out what another means anyway?

Have you ever heard an employee say, "My boss tosses off instructions so fast I never know for sure what he wants me to do or how he wants it done"? Comments such as this illustrate the problems we all face in communicating effectively and precisely. How can we, as senders of a message, be sure the receivers understand? And, as receivers, how can we be sure what we understand is what the sender intended? We must constantly pick a path between over-communication (boring!) and under-communication (confusing!). When employees feel their managers' instructions are too general, they proceed with a feeling of uncertainty. On the other hand, if the manager is too explicit, the employee may feel the manager has no faith in his ability or his intelligence.

In this chapter we look at some of the problems associated with meanings. Some of the key questions explored are: How do we "mean"? How are meanings transferred? What are some traps to avoid?

"That's What I Said, but It Isn't What I Mean"

How do people "mean" anyway? We said in Chapter One that communication is not a product. An idea or information cannot be packaged and handed to the receiver as we can with a packaged product. Then, how do we package an idea in order to transfer it to the receiver? When we discussed this problem with one employee, he said, "I don't worry about all that stuff. I just say what I mean and I mean what I say." This would appear to be an admirable goal, but at the same time, it overlooks the complexity of communicating our meanings. Just how do we say what we mean? It isn't an easy question. Let's look at some of the pitfalls associated with the process.

When two people engage in conversation, what passes between them? When we have asked this question in our training programs, we have received a variety of answers, some of which have been "ideas," "information," "understanding," "words," "feelings," "nonverbal messages," and so on. These answers are all true, but only up to a point. For example, can you take a picture of a word passing from one person to another? (You *can* take a picture of an exchange of a package.) Can you take a picture of a nonverbal message passing between two people? Hardly.

Certainly, you can take pictures of people and their expressions and movements, but what is exchanged between the eyes of the people involved and what is going on inside their heads? When we view communication in a microscopic fashion, we recognize that all that passes between two communicating people are vibrations, either of the air waves, which we call sound, or of the light waves, which we translate into sight. If we can grasp this concept and realize its significance, we can begin to understand some of our communication failures.

When we wish to communicate with another we must encode our idea or thought into verbal and/or nonverbal vibrations. These vibrations are symbols and are, therefore, not as important in themselves as for what they represent. A symbol, simply explained, is something that stands for something else. It represents a concept we have about something such as a thing, person, idea, object, or belief. In general, it is easier for us to think of objects—flags, insignia, brands, trademarks, signs—as being symbols. But words are symbols, too. (In this chapter primary concern will be with words and in Chapter Four we will look more closely at the role of communication without words, or nonverbal communication.)

Words, as symbols, serve an important function, for they provide vehicles through which we can transmit ideas and information, thus creating messages. Remember that words themselves are not the information that we are transmitting. They are not the things, behavior, feelings, or ideas, but only symbols. Before we can use words effectively, we must understand the nature of meaning, the source of messages, and the methods by which we can produce the maximum in understanding.

Meanings Are in People

Words do not have meanings, nor do words contain meaning as a glass might contain water. The "container" concept is one of the most damaging misconceptions about words. Maybe you have said, or heard someone say, "I'll look that word up in the dictionary and see what it means." But dictionaries give us definitions, not meanings. Definitions tell us what most people have agreed the symbol represents. Meaning, on the other hand, is highly individual and personal. Many arguments are fomented and end in frustration only because both parties had different definitions for a word and each was sure his or her meaning was the "right" one. (This was apparently the case in the argument between employees.)

The point should be clear by now that meanings are not inherent in a word or phrase. Nor is the word the idea or object it stands for. What's more, we should avoid the notion that there is a right or wrong relationship between objects and words. The word "desk," for example, performs a function of identifying a certain class of object to persons who have had some experience with furniture labeled "desk." Other words like "table," "podium," "bureau," "pulpit," and "secretary" also refer to this class of objects which may be called "desk." But these words are only groups of letters from the alphabet; if spoken, they are sounds—no more. To find out what they mean we must look inside ourselves because meanings are in people, not in words.

Let's take a closer look at the role words play in establishing meanings. For all of us, hearing or reading the term "desk" causes us to have a picture in our heads. That is, we "see" a desk, but none of us is likely to have exactly the same picture. However, even this picture in our heads does not establish meaning. Suppose someone pointed to a pulpit and said "desk." What would it mean to each of us? Would we share the same meaning? Very unlikely. To one person it might mean something on which to place books or notes while speaking to an audience. To someone else it might mean something sacred and call up feelings of reverence and reluctance to touch it or stand behind it. We would be looking at the same object, but the meaning of that object to each of us would be highly personal because the meaning of anything is inside the person. The meaning we place on it is the result of our experience with the object.

Although words have very private meanings and are inadequate vessels to carry meanings, we have to use them. The relationship of the word to the thing or event is therefore of great importance. There are two ways we can talk about the object, "desk." We can point to the desk or we can use the word-symbol for it. The word is available to the individual whenever he wishes to refer to the object; this is considerably easier than carrying a desk around. Words, however, can never mean something in some absolute way, independent of the people involved in the communication act.

When we grasp the concept that meanings are in people rather than words, we take an entirely different view of the nature of communication. We see the necessity for establishing meanings together. Suppose you went along with us to visit an historical church in which there is a "desk" which we all identify as a "pulpit." Perhaps we have some conversation about it. Later, when we are back home and the "pulpit" is referred to, we all would be able to visualize the particular object. Of course, each of us would not remember exactly the same features or have the identical feelings about it, but there would be overlapping of the pictures in our heads which makes possible a certain level of communication between us.

Creating Meanings Between People

We have attempted to establish two points: (1) meaning is a private affair, and (2) individuals cannot have identical experience in any given situation. If these conclusions are true, how is it possible ever to create meaning between people? *We must accept the probability that no two people can ever completely grasp a meaning exactly in the same way.* Accepting this concept prevents us from always placing the blame for misunderstanding on the other person and continually encourages us to seek ways to clarify messages. By exploring our common experiences, we will find bases for agreement to use certain words as well as words to be avoided.

So far, we have examined some of the major factors that significantly affect how we communicate: the nature of words, symbols, relationships between words and objects, and creation of meanings. Our aim has been to show how words are uncertain vehicles for the transmission of meanings and how communication can become more effective if we create wider areas of commonality. Another way to improve clarity is to look at some of the misperceptions we may experience as communicators.

Intent vs. Content

A woman was driving to the city one day when suddenly a tire of her car went flat. She stopped, and although she was able to change the tire, she hoped someone would stop and help since she was dressed for a speaking engagement. Soon a young man stopped and as he walked up to her he said, "Gotta flat tire?" Now, if the woman heard only the words she might have been irritated and said something like, "You stupid idiot, anyone can see it's a flat!"

Such a response would have guaranteed that she would have changed the tire herself. However, she was smart enough to hear the intent of his message which was, "I see you have a problem, can I help you?" If for some reason we cannot listen between the lines we may hear only the content and completely miss the intent of the message. This may result in hurt feelings and strained relationships.

Talking Past Each Other

Communication has been defined as shooting information at a target and (perhaps) hitting it. But shooting or sending messages is not communicating. Haven't you heard two people talking and realize that they are completely missing each other's point? They may be using the same words, but each has different meanings for them; or they may be using different words which represent the same thing.

Thus, they may think they are in agreement when they are not, or they may believe they are in conflict when actually they agree.

How easy it is to forget that words may be used in more than one way. When we construct messages for our own ears, or virtually talk to ourselves, we cannot expect to get our messages through to another person.

A sensitive communicator does not assume that the other person understands automatically. He or she tries to avoid the problem of talking past someone else by pausing, listening, seeking feedback, then elaborating and paraphrasing.

Lack of Discrimination

Meanings are distorted when a communicator fails to recognize variations, differences, and nuances in words. In Chapter One we introduced the concept of "frozen evaluation," which is the tendency to categorize similar events, objects, or people as all being the same: "All part-time employees are alike"; "All Ford automobiles are the same." When frozen evaluations occur, we fail to separate like objects from one another, overlooking differences, while at the same time overemphasizing similarities. This categorizing, stereotyping, and classifying process stops further discrimination.

Just as we can have frozen evaluations about people or events, we can also have them about words. When we assign one meaning to a word, and only one meaning, we are guilty of limiting the possible variety of meanings a word may have for others. Take for example the word, "work." What does it mean? In a first-grade class the teacher was trying to show her pupils the difference between the words "work" and "recreation." She prepared two pictures for illustration. One was a picture of a man reading a book, to represent recreation, while the other was a picture of a man cutting wood, to symbolize work.

When the pictures were presented to the students they had no difficulty responding with the appropriate words, except for one little girl who continually reversed them. She was so firm in her position that the teacher took her aside to determine the problem. The teacher soon learned that the child's father was a teacher, and when he "worked" he was reading; but he cut wood when the family went camping which was, of course, recreation. Even teachers have to unfreeze their own evaluations of words.

Failure to Allow for Change

Misunderstanding often occurs when we either deliberately or unconsciously spread an evaluation over the future or the past. There is a tendency to treat people and communicate with them on the assumption that they are constants, incapable of past or future change.

The tragedy of this is that our assumptions are generally based on archaic evaluations. Not only do we do this to others, but we can do it to ourselves. Have you ever communicated with people on the basis of your own outdated self-concept? The effective communicator will continually update his or her evaluations and always take a new look at each communication act.

Either/Or Polarization

The ease with which we see everything in strict "black and white," "either/or" terms readily distorts meanings. Instead of examining varying degrees in a situation or event, we are more likely to polarize. We fail to see the gradations or middle ground on a matter. It is all or nothing at all.

Our language is not very helpful in this matter because we do not have very many "middle" words. We can point to gray as the middle point between black and white, but what would be the middle positions between successful and unsuccessful, honest and dishonest, happy and unhappy? Of course there are some situations which are either/or. A person is manager of a business or not. Someone is either a college graduate or not. But for most communication situations, we should look for the middle positions and not force people or ideas into mutually exclusive categories.

Saying All That Can Be Said

An interesting experiment is to take some object, like an apple, and try to say all that can be said about it. It may seem simple, but before reading further, try it. How many items are you able to come up with? How long did it take?

In Chapter Two we discussed the difficulty of understanding the self-concept. One of the points made was that we can never know all there is to know about ourselves or about other people. Sometimes our communication breaks down because we behave as if our perceptions represent all there is to be known.

Perhaps our preoccupation with our own versions of reality leads us to lose objectivity in our perceptions. Reality becomes blurred when we are caught up in our own feelings, thoughts, beliefs, and suppositions. The difficulty arises when, not realizing a discrepancy exists, we misread others and find that they are misreading us.

Fact/Inference Confusion

The heart of many problems of misunderstanding is that the receiver may be confused between a statement of fact and a statement of inference. A statement of fact corresponds directly with what one observes; it can only be made after observation. Such statements do not go beyond what has been observed by someone. By contrast, statements of inference can be made at any time, even before an expected event occurs; they can go well beyond observation, and very often cause misunderstanding and confusion. The chief difficulty is that we fail to perceive that we are making statements of inference and that such statements involve uncertainty.

For example, suppose you walk into the office one day and find the assistant manager sitting with his eyes closed and his feet on the desk. If you, in reporting this to someone else, say, "The assistant manager was sitting with his eyes closed and his feet on the desk," you have made a factual statement. But if, on the other hand, you say, "The assistant manager is goofing off," you are in the realm of inference and you have made a leap from what you saw to making a judgment about what you saw.

Another shortcoming of our language is that it does not offer any clue to the difference between inferential statements and factual ones. Both statements, "Joe has his feet on the desk," and "Joe is goofing off," are declarative sentences and apparently statements of fact. There is no indication that the second statement is judgmental. But a good communicator will carefully discriminate between messages based on inference and those based on observation. It may be that Joe is indeed goofing off, but it also may be that Joe is pursuing a creative idea that will save the business a good deal of money. Any communication based on inferences has a higher probability of being inaccurate or invalid than a statement which confines itself to descriptions of what is observed.

We are not saying that everyone should stop making inferences; we must make them. It is impossible to observe everything, and so we must rely often on other people's thinking or reasoning about what someone has observed. The problem arises when we make inferences and then pass them along to other people as facts.

Come Down off That Abstraction Ladder

Let's suppose you are at a party one evening where you meet an interesting person and engage in polite conversation. He asks what you do. You reply, "I manage a unit of the economic life of the nation." Chances are he will excuse himself and go talk to someone else. But maybe he is interested enough to ask what that means. You then reply, "I manage a distribution system." Your new friend is still puzzled, but if he is intrigued enough he might continue to ask what you mean. Now you answer, "I manage a retail business." This is the first real communication you've given him, but he presses you again. "I manage a food store," you explain. Now he inquires about which one and you finally tell him, "The P & Q at the Westside Shopping Center."

In this hypothetical conversation we have watched an individual "coming down the abstraction ladder." Look again at the words used to describe your place of employment:

A unit of the economic life of the nation
A distribution system
A retail business
A food store
A P & Q Store

The first statement is almost meaningless, while the last one is very specific and concrete. A closer look at the abstracting process shows how it affects meaning and understanding.

Abstraction is our selective response to our environment. We are surrounded by countless events, happenings, stimuli. From these we select certain ones or parts of them, which we remember or which have meanings for us. We also ignore many of them. A significant portion of this process is carried on in the subconscious or at the inattentive level. Our responses to certain stimuli frequently are pushed into the subconscious from habit. We do not see, feel, hear, taste, touch, or respond just in terms of an object itself, but in relation to our previous experiences. Our brain is conditioned to abstract certain qualities and leave out or supply others. In this sense, abstracting is related to the process of perception.

The more information we give the receiver, the fewer choices he or she has in meaning selection. If we go back to our illustration of the job description and place of employment, notice that each step down the abstraction ladder reduces the choices. Even the highest level reduces some choices. When you indicate you work within "a unit of the economic life of the nation," there has been some limitation placed on the scope of your employment. For example, the receiver can rule out the military or a nonprofit organization. When you come down a step and say "a distribution system," you have further reduced the options. For example, the receiver knows you are not in manufacturing. At the next step, "a retail business," you have again reduced the extent of the choices. When you say you "work at a food store" and finally at a "P & Q in the Westside Shopping Center," you have decreased the possibility for the receiver to the point where understanding is greatly enhanced.

When communication is effective, it reduces the number of choices available to a receiver. In other words, if you can give the receiver enough information that is concrete, he or she can, through the process of elimination, receive the intended message.

Although we have pointed out the dangers inherent in abstraction, there is another side of the coin. All abstracting is not bad. In fact, like inference-making, it is a very necessary function in human communication. It is important to remember that we and everyone we communicate with are constantly abstracting and distilling the essence because we cannot say all there is to say about any given event or idea.

Without common words for things, ideas, and events, there could not be communication. If we didn't have a common word for the thing we call "automobile," or "car," we would have to use a different word for each vehicle we see. But the word "car" is very abstract. If you tell an employee to go out to the parking lot and roll up the windows in your car, and he did not know what your car looked like, you would have to "come off the abstraction ladder" if the employee is ever able to carry out your instructions.

Putting Words Together

So far in this chapter we have been concerned with how we transmit words or symbols in ways which create meanings. We have looked at a variety of factors associated with this problem. In this section our concern will be with tailoring messages or how to put words together to form messages that are shaped for the message receiver.

Regardless of what we say or how we say it, some messages get through and produce meaning in the receiver. But what is vital to communication is arranging our message so that we get the desired response rather than just any response.

Consider this manager's instructions to an employee for typing a quarterly report: "Ruth, here is the rough draft of the quarterly report which must be retyped. You'll need 20-pound letterhead for the original, three copies should be enough—for Bob Mason, Dale Callaway, and Joan Fletcher—they should be onionskin. If you are unsure of the format, refer to the file of previous reports or to the company manual. I believe it has some suggestions on this. Oh, by the way, leave page 12 blank; Floyd Barker is preparing a data sheet on inventory breakage. I'll need the final report to take with me to the district meeting day after tomorrow. Better send a copy to Pete Goldman, too. Let's see, I guess that's everything. I'll be out the rest of the day and will be in only a few hours tomorrow. If you don't hear from Barker today, call him and tell him you must have his report. Remember, if you have any questions, don't hesitate to ask; this report's got to be correct to the very last detail. Good luck; see you tomorrow." The manager leaves the office.

It is, of course, obvious that this is not very effective communication. The manager has probably left a very confused woman back at the office. Would you like to speculate on the probability that the report will be "correct to the very last detail"?

Let's analyze this communication by looking at possible problems. See if you can spot the problem before reading the analysis. The following are some possible problems:

1. Ruth's frame of reference is not considered. The manager used words she may not understand or for which she may not have the same referents.
2. Instructions are poorly organized and hard to follow.
3. Much of the information is unnecessary.
4. The manager constructed the message for himself; he was too high on the abstraction ladder.

If you had to pick one from the list, which would it be? Clearly, each contributes to the ineffectiveness of this message, but not to the same degree. The first problem could contribute to misunderstanding since the frame of reference in communication is always important. Apparently, Ruth has been in her position a relatively short time (or at least has never had to type the quarterly report before), so some of the language may not be clear to her.

If you chose the second problem, however, consider yourself an expert. This is the key problem; the message goes in circles. For example, how many copies were requested? What is the absolute deadline for completion of the report? When should she contact Barker about his report? Should she type the report and leave page 12 blank or have Barker's part before she comes to page 12? What if Barker's report won't fit on one page? The manager could have avoided much of this confusion and possible distortion of his message if his points had been covered without jumping back and forth. Four points were important: typing instructions, including format; instructions on the inventory breakage insert; information on how many copies and who will receive them; and the exact deadline for completion of the report.

The amount of information, as number three above suggests, is not the cause of the confusion; rather, it is the lack of any organization. The last statement exposes a significant contributing factor, however. There seems to be no concern for Ruth, no attempt to adjust to her world, or any awareness of her as a person. This message does not appear to be prepared for a specific person. The manager seems to be communicating with himself, almost in a stream-of-consciousness way. He has not placed himself in the position of the receiver. He assumes Ruth's world is the same as his. However, if the report is improperly prepared or late, who do you expect will get the blame?

Let's take a contrasting example in which the manager might be the receiver of a message rather than the sender. One morning, you open your mail and find the following memo from your superior:

"After extensive study, the decision has been made, with reluctance, I assure you, to request that each and every manager—with clear and commensurate planning—raise his sights and motivate his subordinates to increase the gross income by at least 10 percent above the present output.

"We are naturally proud of the substantial increase that each of you has been able to realize through your dedication as well as that of your employees. However, the circumstances which now exist in the economic arena; that is, the economic upturn which was predicted and not forthcoming, has created a need for an increase in our gross income, which will permit us to remain competitive, and hopefully, to maintain our present level of solvency."

What is this all about? You and your business need to raise more money, right? But how? Where would you start? Would you be able to carry out these instructions with a high degree of confidence?

What's wrong with this communication? Three things are readily evident. First, the language is very abstract and indirect. Second, its tone is pompous, seemingly more concerned with impressing than with communicating. Third, the organization of the points, although in a certain order, is lost in all the excess verbiage. The use or misuse of language obscures the real message. The intent is obscured by the content.

Remember that when we communicate we cannot transmit meaning, only symbols. Before any communication takes place, the sender should answer six simple questions and shape the message accordingly. Three apply to the sender: (1) What do I intend to communicate? (2) What will I actually communicate, sometimes in spite of my good intentions? (3) What will I really mean, or what will be the emotional impact of what I communicate? The other three questions apply to the receivers: (1) What do they expect to hear? (2) What will they actually hear at times, despite what is said? (3) How will they feel about what they hear?

This chapter has explored factors affecting the process of meaning which cause communication breakdowns. Acquiring and using meanings and language are learned behaviors, influenced largely through interaction with others. Language is only a tool which must be understood if it is to be used properly. A great deal of practice is needed, but every time we open our mouths to speak we have a chance to work with this tool and perfect it.

Think of words as rocks in a stream; you can use them as stepping stones to get to the other side or they can become stumbling blocks that only prove you're all wet.

4
Communicating Without Words

As you enter your office one day, you find your assistant manager talking on the telephone. Waiting for him to complete the call, you begin to tune into the conversation. Apparently he is telling someone how to find the store. As he talks, he points with his finger to indicate directions and turns, and when he pauses to listen, the assistant manager shakes his head from side to side suggesting to you that the message is not understood by the caller. He repeats the instructions with more gestures and a variety of bodily movements. This time, when he listens he moves his head in an up-and-down motion, indicating that the other party now seems to understand.

After the call is completed and the assistant manager is out of the office, you sit down at your desk and begin to work. Remembering the call, you are amused at all the assistant manager's wasted gestures. You smile to yourself and wonder if he received training in using effective gestures for the telephone at the managerial workshop he attended recently.

You get busy, and the incident fades in your memory until suddenly it is recalled as a result of a telephone conversation you have. The call is a routine one from the district manager, but after the business matters are discussed, he asks about your vacation. Since your recent vacation was a particularly enjoyable and exciting one, your whole manner changes as you tell him about the trip. You tell the district manager about the great time you and the family had camping and fishing in the mountains. You describe with delight the fish you caught and those you almost caught. You tell how one of your children fell into the cold, swift mountain stream, and you had to wade into the water to rescue him.

Suddenly you realize that throughout this conversation you have been gesturing continually, demonstrating the size of the fish, pointing, and so forth. You are no longer amused by your assistant manager's behavior and wonder why it is that we persist in using unseen gestures in our telephone conversations.

In our speech-oriented culture it is easy to regard the process of communication as an entirely verbal act. After all, our schools encouraged us to become more conscious of words than of non-words. Remember how much time you spent increasing your verbal vocabulary? You learned to read, write, and spell; but can you recall spending any time on increasing your nonverbal vocabulary or in understanding how people communicate without words?

As important as the language of words is, it is only a small part of the total language we use in communicating with others. One of the most startling research findings in the field of communication is that in face-to-face communication, no more than 35 percent of the social meaning comes from words. *That leaves 65 percent to be carried by nonverbal messages.*

The purpose of this chapter is to investigate the ways in which we communicate without words through the various aspects of nonverbal communication. Before we begin, however, we would like to stress that we feel the subject is too complex and too variable to be reduced to the pat answers found in some of today's "how-to" books. We will not set forth a systematic code or offer ten easy lessons to "psych out" another person's secrets through analyzing nonverbal behavior. We don't believe in making categorical assertions such as, "When people sit with their legs crossed or their arms folded it means they are withdrawn or introverted." It may mean that and then again, it may not.

The successful communicator needs to be aware of nonverbal messages and, wherever possible, learn to understand their significance. From infancy on, we have been "reading" and responding to nonverbal clues. It was our first language, long before we could interpret or form words. We looked for and responded to our mother's touch and smile. But our understanding was basically at the subconscious level; it is usually quite difficult to sort out subtle and rapid behaviors for what they mean. The better we know people, however, the more accurate are our interpretations of their nonverbal messages.

We Can't NOT Communicate

When two people are placed within sensory range of each other, it is impossible for them not to communicate. There really is no such thing as noncommunication because all behavior has some kind of message value. To illustrate this concept, we sometimes ask an individual in our training programs to stand before the group and try his or her best not to communicate anything at all to the audience. People find this impossible to do. Even if they stand absolutely still or turn their backs, a message comes through. If they smile or frown or move, however slightly, or if they refuse even to look at the group, they have still communicated. Since all behavior communicates something, and we are behaving in some way all of the time, we are communicating constantly whether we wish to or not. Both activity and inactivity transmit messages which influence others and, therefore, can rightly be called communication.

"What do you mean I'm communicating?" one man asked us. "Let's suppose I go into a restaurant and sit down and look straight ahead. I talk to no one, I eat my meal, pay my check and leave. I have spoken to no one but the waitress. How can this possibly be communication?" For one thing he has communicated to the people around him that he does not wish to communicate. This behavior is just as much an interchange as an animated conversation might be.

Communication occurs regardless of whether it is intentional, conscious, or successful. Whether they go along to emphasize words, to supplement words, or are independent from words, nonverbal messages are very important keys.

Physical Communication

The most obvious nonverbal messages come to and from the body. As communication receivers, we use all our senses. We see another's facial expression; we hear a particular tone of voice; we feel the touch of a hand on our shoulder; we taste the seasonings used by a gourmet cook; and we smell a person's perfume or lotion. As both senders and receivers, we are aware that how the body looks and how it moves are important. We are affected by a person's style of clothing, neatness, coloring, and grooming. We are influenced by a person's posture, the way he or she walks, stands, and moves. Is the person graceful or clumsy? Does he or she stand tall or slouch?

Physical movements may be overt such as big, forceful gestures or they may be subtle like the lifting of an eyebrow. Physical activity is such an integral part of our verbal activity that often we are completely unaware that we are performing it.

For example, suppose in the middle of a very busy day an employee comes to see you about a problem. You discuss the problem, and between you, it is solved. But the employee lingers and turns the conversation to social matters. Inwardly, you want to terminate the discussion and get back to work, but outwardly you are polite and attentive. Then you move forward in your chair to a more upright position and begin to straighten papers on your desk. Whether these movements are subconscious or deliberate, they betray your real feelings and should signal the employee that it is time to go. Unless the employee is insensitive or too preoccupied with personal problems, the conversation most likely will come to a close by tacit, mutual agreement.

As one method of illustrating our dependency upon bodily movements to supplement our verbal communication, we have sometimes asked trainees to attempt to produce sarcastic messages which we put on videotape. It was a surprise to us how many people relied entirely on facial expressions rather than tone of voice to communicate sarcasm. When the picture was turned off and only the audio portion played, an entirely different message came through. Even when this was pointed out, these same people were unable to put sarcasm into their voices; they simply relied on facial expressions to convey emotions. In situations where the receivers of their messages could not see their faces, such as over the telephone, the message intent would not get through. It is, then, important to be able to use all aspects of nonverbal communication in order to adapt to conditions and circumstances.

Certainly, all bodily behavior communicates something to the receiver. However, we must guard against making generalizations or stereotypes which are based, not on the evidence before us, but on our own past experiences with various individuals. A person who wears a grumpy face is not necessarily a grumpy person. You've heard people say, "Oh, sure, he looks like a sourpuss, but once you get to know him, you'll find he has a great sense of humor." We must be willing to accept the variations in human behavior as we read nonverbal messages, and we must remember how the "deadpan," expressionless face is a definite asset in joke-telling and poker-playing.

To illustrate how physical behavior can influence the meaning of the verbal behavior, study the following drawings.

Imagine each one of these fellows is saying, "That's just fine." What is your meaning for each expression? How do you arrive at

---

Figure 3

That's just fine.

That's just fine.

That's just fine.

That's just fine.

---

these meanings and what cues suggest the changes and variations from figure to figure?

These drawings give us a chance to demonstrate one more aspect of nonverbal communication. By our nonverbal expressions, we send the receiver a message or an indication about how to interpret the content of the message we are sending. As you send a message, it is very likely that you will communicate your own evaluation of the content, your interest, your excitement, your intention. Implicitly or explicitly you tell the receiver how to react to the communication. These nonverbal instructions are received at the same time as the verbal message arrives, and, as in the case of our drawings, they tell you whether the message is sincere of if you are to interpret the words that suggest "fine" to mean that it is really "not fine."

Visual Sending and Receiving

Our ears serve only one function in communication—to receive sounds. In nonverbal communication, however, our eyes do double duty. They both receive and send messages. Consider the following illustration.

At the poker table, an inexperienced player may inadvertently betray too much for his own good. Sometimes he places his chips in the middle of the table, while at other times he keeps them on his side of the table. In one instance he may sit close to the table and at other times lean back and away. During one hand he may move quickly to place his bet while at other times he may move more slowly and with deliberation. A professional gambler would be aware of such variations in an opponent's behavior and would be able to estimate when he has a winning hand and when he is less certain. An excellent poker player not only maintains the traditional "poker face," but also constantly assumes the same posture, always placing the chips in the same location as he bets, and moving at the same speed. This uniform and neutral behavior increases the likelihood that minimal information will be transmitted to the other players, and they will thus not be able to tell if he is bluffing or not.

The above illustrates the importance of gross bodily movement and how it can communicate to a person who is aware of the significance of such activity. However, there is another, more subtle dimension that is often overlooked. An experienced poker player may very well be able to control overt behavior but have less success in controlling involuntary movements. Professional poker players report that they can read their opponents by watching for variations in the size of the eye's pupil.

Today there is sufficient evidence to support the idea that our pupils dilate according to the degree of liking or disliking a given subject. For example, there are magicians who claim that when doing card tricks they can spot a card preselected by a volunteer subject because his pupils will enlarge when he sees the card again. Similarly, street vendors watch the potential buyer's eyes so that they will be able to tell when he sees something he likes. The vendor will then use this information in pricing the particular item.

Expressions of people's eyes and the dilating of pupils may seem a long way from the world of the manager, but there is evidence to support the notion that we respond to the dilation of other people's eyes without even knowing it.

Experimenters have shown a group of photographs to male subjects. Among the pictures would be two of the face of the same beautiful woman. The pictures were identical in every detail except that the woman's pupils had been retouched so that they were enlarged in one picture and very small in the other. The men were asked to look at the pictures one at a time. While they were looking at the pictures, the subject's eyes were being photographed. In every case, when the men looked at the picture of the face with the large pupils, the men's own pupils enlarged in size.

When the men were questioned later, most of them believed the pictures were identical, although a few reported that one face had seemed somehow softer or prettier. Since in not a single case had the men noticed the difference in the eyes, it seems clear that the enlarged pupil may be attractive at some subliminal level. This may be one explanation of why we sometimes have a feeling that we definitely like or dislike someone we have seen but have not even met.

Eye contact is an important element of communication. We are more likely to trust those who look us directly in the eye, because it is a nonverbal indication that they are telling the truth. On the other hand, people do not like the feeling of being stared at. When a speaker looks us squarely in the eyes, perhaps singling us out of a group of people for special attention, we get the message that he is speaking directly to us and that he cares whether we are listening and comprehending. But if the direct glance becomes a stare, we start to squirm and wonder if there might be something unusual about ourselves (a spot on a tie, a slip showing?) that calls for such uncomfortable scrutiny. In our culture it is considered impolite, inappropriate, and threatening to have people stare at us. We should be aware, however, that in other cultures, the meaning is different.

The concept of the "evil eye" is prevalent in many cultures, and it is not uncommon to come across the belief that a gaze from some people can injure or even cause death. Some believe that the possession of this strange ocular power was acquired in a mystical pact with the devil. Although it is easy to scoff at such primitive beliefs, it is interesting to note that as late as 1957, a congressional investigation found that some American employers hired individuals to come into their organizations just to stand around and stare at the work force. It was believed that such activity kept workers "in line."

We have been investigating the function of the eyes in sending messages primarily. Now we would like to examine more carefully the role our eyes play in receiving messages.

Of all our senses, we rely most heavily upon sight for the major source of information about people and the world around us. When managers say, "I'd better go out on the floor and *see* how things are going," it is one indication of how much they rely upon vision as a means of collecting information.

Managers are well aware of the influence on the customer of packaging and display arrangements. We know that a change in color can change not only how we feel but how we move as well. For years, architects and designers have been providing box-like rooms with soothing colors for hospitals and nursing homes. But we know today that people can suffer from boredom and lack of stimuli when they are confined to a hospital bed, and that color and variety often improve both morale and health.

The human eye is a miraculous instrument. But it is controlled by the brain, and like the brain it has a tendency to wander. When we consider all the possible things we might look at in our environment, it is no wonder we have taught our eyes to be selective. Something has to "catch" our eye to get our attention—something bright, unusual, or moving. Also, we sometimes see what we expect to see instead of "reality." Ask witnesses to an accident or an unusual event to describe what they saw and marvel at the differences in the accounts. To turn the old saying around, "believing is seeing."

Hearing and Being Heard

In Chapter Six we will spend more time discussing the art of listening. However, since sounds are a significant aspect of nonverbal communication, they need to be mentioned here as well. Noise is such a constant factor in our environment, we are apt to take it for granted; yet it can influence our moods and effectiveness at work. Efficiency experts have discovered that workers can better tolerate the steady sounds of a factory going full blast than sudden bursts of noise like those created by typewriters and computers. Teenagers have argued for years that they could study better with the radio on, and it seems that they are right if the radio hum is steady enough to blank out irregular sounds around them.

Since our voices are such an integral part of our verbal communication, we often overlook the nonverbal component. The voice, however, can reflect much of our inner reactions, attitudes, and feelings. Such things as pitch, quality, volume, rate, and rhythm all influence the verbal messages we send.

In an employment interview, the applicant might say all the right things, but the way he says them may cost him the job. For example, he may say in positive words that he is interested in the position, that he will work hard, and that he believes very much in what the company is doing. But the interviewer may notice that his bland, expressionless voice and face do little to confirm his verbalized enthusiasm; he may decide intuitively that the applicant doesn't mean what he says.

Very few of us have any clear perceptions of how our voices sound to others. The first time we hear our own voices on audio- or videotape, we are likely to say, "That's not me. Do I sound like that?" We are referring to vocal quality and pitch which our own ears receive differently than our listeners do. So, too, the nonverbal clues connected with our voices are often unknown to us.

Sometimes we use tonal qualities to send two-edged messages. We generally do this when we wish to convey heavy sarcasm which we can blandly deny when we are confronted. The simple formula for this, when the other person protests or takes exception to what we have said, is to say something like, "But all I said was . . ." and use an innocent tone instead of the original negative one.

For example, when a husband comes home one night, his wife tells him in a very exasperated fashion, "I really like the way we get to go out so often." He responds, incredulously, with, "What do you mean? Why, last Saturday we went to the track meet at the University and two nights ago we went to a movie." Her reply may be something like, "All I said was that I like the way we get to go out so often," only this time it is with a neutral tone of voice. Husbands and wives have had to learn to hear and respond to all kinds of nonverbal messages.

Those of us who work in jobs where we constantly meet the public have a special problem of sounding sincere and responsive. For example, the cashier's verbal contact of, "Good day," as a customer comes to pay the bill may have little responsiveness the thirtieth time compared to the first few times. It can sound as if it is a tape recording which never varies from customer to customer and is mechanical and routine. We do not wish to minimize the importance of the verbal message, but without the feeling or nonverbal tone of expression that should accompany our verbal communication, mere words often miss the mark and leave the listener confused or even hostile.

It is possible to say something negative while at the same time making the statement positive nonverbally. Suppose a close friend whom you have not seen recently surprises you one day by visiting you at work. Seeing your old friend, you may spring to your feet and say something like, "Well you old son of a . . .!" as you slap him on the back. Although you have made a disparaging comment about his ancestry, you have expressed it in such a way that it communicates extreme liking. In our North American culture, it is difficult for a man to reveal great affection for another man, and so two men who are fond of one another often use negative verbal messages while at the same time communicating very affectionately on a nonverbal level. Once again, it should be pointed out that the important message was not what was said (the content), but how it was said (the intent of the communication).

The Communication of Space

Where you sit or stand during a communicative interaction also has message value. There is a significant difference between the message that comes across from someone who sits behind a desk and one that is implied when a person comes around a desk and sits closer to a visitor. The desk itself can create a barrier which subtly signifies status and remoteness. This physical distance between persons tells a great deal about the nature of their communication as well as their relationship.

In old war movies, have you ever seen a German or Russian officer portrayed in his office with his desk against the wall so that he is fully exposed to his visitors? On the contrary, the officer usually sits behind a huge desk in front of which his visitor must stand. (Of course, this may only be the movie-maker's attempt to bring out the stereotype of unconcerned and distant leadership in an authoritarian culture.) Speaking of movies, the reason foreign films often seem stilted is that only the words can be translated—not the nonverbal aspects the original actors put into them.

Each of us has our own private territory; we can become extremely uncomfortable when people intrude upon our private space. To learn about this particular phenomenon, try moving gradually in on another person. When you cross the invisible line that marks their "territory," he or she will probably begin to inch away or change position in order not to be quite so close to you.

Crowded elevators are notorious for violating one's personal space, for there we are frequently forced to stand embarrassingly close to strangers, in positions that would not be assumed spontaneously if we were in a large, open space. Closeness, implying intimacy and liking, is socially unacceptable with a stranger. The next time you find yourself in a crowded elevator, observe the behavior of your fellow travelers. Many will stand as if they were drawing themselves inward, with arms close to their bodies, trying desperately not to touch those standing next to them. They compensate for this excessive closeness by avoiding each others' eyes and staring at the floor indicator signal. If we were actually to face the other people and look directly into their eyes, we would not only make them very uncomfortable, but probably also would give the impression of being strange or possibly even maladjusted.

The anthropologist, Edward Hall, has made extensive studies of the phenomenon of space and what it communicates. From his work, a field known as "proxemics" has developed. Hall explains the word he has coined as "the interrelated observations and theories of man's use of space as a specialized elaboration of culture."[1]

Hall's work has been concerned with the misunderstandings that can develop because people from different cultures handle space in different ways. He has learned, for example, that for two unacquainted male North Americans, the comfortable distance to stand for conversation is about two feet apart. People from many other cultures, however, prefer to stand much closer, which can create a problem when they do not understand each other's preferences. An individual who likes to stand closer when communicating and who tends to move into what is to him a proper talking distance may be considered "pushy" by others. On the other hand, some people may

---

1. Edward T. Hall, *The Hidden Dimension* (New York: Doubleday and Co., 1966), p.1.

seem "standoffish" or cold to an individual who likes closeness in the interaction.

It is important to understand that North Americans live in a primarily noncontact culture. Physical closeness usually communicates to most North Americans that people are either courting or conspiring. Although there is no absolute method for accurately interpreting distance, the following observations seem valuable: When the distance between two people is 18 inches or less, this is the space for very intimate talk and a discussion of business matters would be regarded as inappropriate. At this range, people communicate not only by space and words, but also by touch, smell, body heat, and so forth. When people stand from a foot and a half to three feet apart, this is still considered a personal distance. A close friend can stand within this space without being offensive. Many husbands have been confronted by angry wives who accused them of letting another woman stand too close, and, therefore, to enter that territory that wives regard as appropriate only for them to occupy.

When the distance is increased, from about four to five feet, it is still accepted as a personal distance appropriate for discussing personal matters, but rarely are intimate matters discussed in this proximity. When we move out from four to seven feet, the social distance has changed considerably. This is the space that generally is used in offices or work situations. However, when a manager stands from four to seven feet from a subordinate and looks down at him or her, it may very well have a domineering effect. When the distance is increased from seven to twelve feet, we are in more of a formal conversation. We can use such objects as desks or furniture to separate individuals from us to maintain this relationship. Beyond twelve feet, we move into the more formal public speaking situation.

Another unstated rule about space is illustrated when two people are standing, talking together in public. They generally stand in such a fashion that they assume the ground they are standing on is temporarily their joint territory and that others will not intrude. If two customers stand together talking, and you are approaching, you will attempt to skirt the edges of the conversational grouping and will lower your head markedly as you go by. If it is necessary to come between the two people in conversation, you will do it apologetically. If you fail to apologize, you will be considered rude and gauche.

In a staff meeting it is not uncommon at all for managers to choose the seat that signifies the most status. They will almost automatically take a chair at the end of a rectangular table. If the meeting is in their office, and they remain behind the desk with their staff sitting before them, this is an extreme example of maintaining distance as an authoritarian stance with the staff. (Of course, some offices are so small or so crowded there isn't much choice of arrangements. Managers should be aware of how attitudes are communicated however, and make the best possible use of whatever facilities are available.)

When two people expect to compete they usually will sit opposite one another; whereas, when they expect to cooperate they tend to sit side by side. For ordinary conversation they may sit at right angles. This is also seen in most negotiation sessions when the teams invariably line up facing one another across the conference table.

The way managers use space in their interactions with subordinates plays a vital role in the effectiveness of their communication. When you choose a particular distance, you are signaling how intimate you wish to be, the status that you wish to communicate, the power you have over the individual, and how formal or informal you wish the interaction to be. A careful examination of the use of space throughout the establishment should also prove useful. One manager, for example, studied the behavior of customers waiting to pay their bills and discovered quite a bit of line-jumping going on, to the great annoyance of the other customers. The manager decided he didn't have much chance of reforming the pushy people of the world, but he could redesign the area to make line-jumping physically impossible.

Communicating Through the Use of Time

Just as space can communicate volumes, the way we utilize our time also reveals important data. Have you ever been kept waiting for an appointment? How did you feel? How did it affect the quality of the interaction when it finally occurred? If you are exactly on time for an appointment, it can reveal something about you and about your attitude of the importance of the situation. Who waits for whom and for how long communicates many things about a relationship. Most organizations have developed informal tolerance ranges for lateness. If we keep people waiting beyond the acceptable tolerance range, we insult them.

The handling of promptness or lateness, however, can vary with the subculture and with the function of a particular meeting. If you are having a meeting with the executive vice-president of your firm, you will most likely arrive well in advance so that you will not run the risk of keeping such an important individual waiting. Yet, you will probably be less concerned about promptness if you have an appointment with one of your subordinates.

There are other dimensions to the communicative value of time, such as the rate at which we speak, move, or gesture, which can tell much about our inner intensity and feeling. The speed with which we walk can tell others our age, attitude, feelings, character—even the state of our health.

An effective manager considers these communication dimensions when making personnel assignments. For example, in a department store, the salesperson who stands behind a counter on the main floor sometimes is called upon to handle a number of customers simultaneously. It is therefore important for this person to be able to maintain a flexible and fast interaction tempo. A salesperson who sells high fashions, on the other hand, often must wait around, making small talk while the customer tries on clothes. This salesperson must be able to sense when the customer responds to a particular garment so that she can move in and make the sale. Although the second clerk's use of time is vastly different from that of the sales clerk on the first floor, it is, nevertheless, quite effective for the situation.

As a manager, you can control the timing of your messages. Whenever possible, try to have the message reach the receivers when they are most likely to accept it positively. If your employees are expecting a message at a given time, punctuality becomes an important issue. If the announcement is late, it may very well have an undesirable effect on the message itself and perhaps communicate something you do not intend. A surefire way of creating hostility is to let your messages reach different people at different times. If part of the work force gets the word before others do, much anxiety and frustration can result.

Contradictory Messages

Let's say the district office has assigned you a manager-trainee. In welcoming the trainee, you say something like the following: "We are all equal here and can express our feelings openly. I want you always to let your feelings be known and especially to me. Let me know if you have reservations about anything or feel that something is wrong. My door is always open, and I want you to feel free to come in anytime or ask me any questions."

Verbally, you have issued a warm welcome. But let's also say that while you spoke, you glanced at your watch several times, and you kept the desk between you and the trainee. The trainee will also get your nonverbal messages which contradict the verbal. He or she might conclude you are trying to be a nice person, but you really don't mean it. In other words, the trainee feels that it will be wise not to be too open with you about problems, and he certainly will not feel free to visit you in your office. The trainee may sense that there is an invisible barrier across your "open door."

This interaction is an example of inconsistency between our words and our behavior. In the above example, the trainee received two conflicting impressions and had to make a decision about which was the real message. As usually happens, the trainee decided that the nonverbal message was the one to be trusted. Because it is spontaneous, a non-verbal message is difficult to fake.

Suppose you have just shaken hands with a friend, and the friend tells you that he feels fine. As he is telling you this, you notice that he quickly looks away, and you realize that his hand felt cold and clammy. You also see that he exhibits a kind of offhand manner, and that he has steered the conversation away from himself and on to some other subject.

In this instance, although you heard your friend say that he felt fine, you have observed certain bodily manifestations and movements and the absence of a direct gaze that strongly communicate the opposite impression. Had you been talking to the same person on the telephone, you would not have seen these reactions, but if you know him well enough you might possibly have discerned a characteristic in the tone or pitch of his voice that you have learned to associate with the words, "I am not fine." But you could not be absolutely sure of this. Only by personally observing the nonverbal signs are you able to comprehend his total message. In this case, the nonverbal message was strong enough to obscure and negate the verbal message contained in the words, "I am fine."

If our communication is to be effective, nonverbal and verbal messages should reinforce each other and form an honest, integrated whole. It is true that some of these mixed, contradictory communications result from the requirement of the social situations in which we find ourselves. Such statements as, "We are glad to see you"; "So glad you could come"; and "You're looking well today" are required amenities and we can surely be forgiven if we don't put our whole hearts into them. But hypocrites are often exposed by their nonverbal clues. Have you ever seen a politician stand before the voters with chest proudly thrust forward, posture erect, and in a booming voice declare, "When I am elected I will be your humble servant!" His whole demeanor, his manner of dress, the props surrounding him all indicate high status and a dominant position. You are hardly likely to believe that the candidate is capable of being a truly humble servant of the people or that he has any intention of trying.

In this chapter, we have discussed the role of nonverbal communication and how it can be harnessed to increase our effectiveness as communicators. We hope managers will be motivated to take a new look at their operations and analyze the intended and unintended messages that greet their customers' eyes and ears. Don't forget the smells from the bakery, the kitchen, or the candy shop, or the absence of a sales clerk when ten customers want attention.

Managers who have a keen awareness of the communicative significance of nonverbal messages will not only ensure accurate communication of their own feelings but also will be able to understand and relate effectively to the messages that they receive from their staff. Managers who disregard nonverbal clues may find themselves frequently misunderstood and frustrated. They may have the impression that the staff are not aware of the significance of messages, that they do not listen carefully, or even that they are simply unconcerned. Managers may obtain dramatically different results when they become fully aware of the fact that the way something is said is just as important as what is said.

5
Feedback and Understanding

In the last two chapters we were concerned with verbal and nonverbal messages. As communicators, we package our ideas, or messages, in either verbal or nonverbal containers. The purpose of this chapter is to determine how we "unwrap" these "packages" and reveal the meanings they contain. We will also discuss how these messages are used to create understanding and how they affect behavior.

In Chapter One we explored some of the conceptions and misconceptions about communication. One of these was the illusion that since communication appears so simple and since everybody does it, it is easy to believe that we all communicate effectively. Most people tend to take for granted that they are being understood when talking with another. However, the fact is that in any given conversation complete understanding is very rare. The difficulty arises when we are so concerned with what we are saying that we fail to read the reactions from the receiver.

Think of the last meeting you attended; let's make it a policy-making group. How often do you recall someone holding up his or her own argument long enough to say, "I think you said ...," or, "Did you mean ...," or, "What I heard you say was ..."? In most meetings of this kind, the fast-moving conversation keeps us so busy organizing our own replies that we don't take the necessary time to make sure we know what we are replying to. If you are like most people, you use your listening time to structure your own argument or response and completely tune out what the other person is saying. When you do this, you are more concerned with the encoding process of communication than with the decoding process.

For example, let's look at the following hypothetical conversation between a manager and the supervisor of the night crew. For this conversation, Dave is a manager and Larry the night supervisor. It is morning when they meet.

Dave: Larry, you just can't believe what happened to me last night! Let me tell you about ...

Larry: Okay, fine. You know, Dave, things aren't going well on the night shift. Unless I can get some reliable workers ...

Dave: When I got home last night everything exploded in my face. First of all, the wife had an accident with the car and this guy calls up ...

Larry: If I don't get a full and reliable staff pretty soon you're going to come in one morning and find ...

Dave: On top of that the school called and said our oldest boy had ditched school and ...

Larry: And besides the inefficient workers that I have, the deliveries are late and they're getting later every night and ...

Dave: Then my youngest kid fell off his bicycle and we had to take him to ...

Larry: Yeah, things sure are rough.

Dave: They sure are.

This dialogue is exaggerated purposely (but not much) to demonstrate how two people can be engaged in conversation and yet completely bypass each other. Perhaps you have heard similar conversations or even participated in some. Dave and Larry were more concerned about the messages they were sending than those being sent to them. They were not reacting to or understanding each other's messages, but only waiting their turn to speak.

When a situation like this develops, we are not talking to each other; we are merely talking. The talking described in this example was not interaction because there was no feedback between the two individuals. Each individual was operating completely independently of the other. Therefore, it cannot be considered useful communication. Instead of communication, we had intersecting monologues.

What we are highlighting here is the direction of communication flow—its one-wayness or two-wayness. No matter what the message intent, or content, no matter how much physical or psychological "noise" interferes, no matter what code is used or what network is involved, the sender can talk to the receiver this way:

$$S \rightarrow R$$

or the sender can talk this way:

$$S \rightleftarrows R$$

Either the sender talks and the receiver merely listens, which is one-way communication, or the sender talks and the receiver talks back, which provides two-way communication.

Creating Meanings With Feedback

As communicators, we seek to elicit some kind of response or understanding in those with whom we communicate. The simple model of communication discussed in Chapter One, Figure 2 is an illustration of the process of feedback in the communicative system. Feedback is necessary to complete the communication loop and to provide within the model a process that will allow for the verification of meaning from the receiver back to the sender. In human communication there is a need for some system by which we can correct, when necessary, what we transmitted. By knowing the results of our communication we can either alter or correct the message so that we can achieve our desired goal, or response, from the receiver.

Have you ever had the experience of writing to a friend who is planning to visit you to give him the instructions for driving to your home? You write very carefully and precisely the necessary instructions, mail them to your friend, and then wait for his arrival. However, when your friend arrives in your town and searches for your house, he can't seem to find it and has to call and ask for additional information. You explain again how to get to your house; maybe you even give up and drive out to meet him and lead him to your place.

Then, you discuss what happened. Why was he unable to find your home by following your instructions? He may very well produce your letter and show what he did as the result of your directions. When you see the letter, you realize that some key data were omitted and that you had assumed your friend had an understanding of a location of a turn which he didn't possess. What happened was that you communicated from *your* frame of reference rather than from *his*. This caused you to overlook the significant information which you take for granted but which someone else would need in order to understand. In this example, communication broke down because there was no feedback from the receiver to the sender and there was no corrective mechanism in the system to prevent an inaccurate interpretation.

Let's look at another example. One day all the managers receive a memo from the district manager, requesting them to "submit a list of needs for next year." None of the managers asks the district manager what is meant by "needs," yet each manager prepares a list and submits it. The district manager is upset with the information he receives. He had expected data on space problems but instead got information about personnel matters from some managers and data on budgetary allocations from others. Since the space problem had been discussed at a recent managers' meeting, the district manager just assumed the managers knew what was meant in the memo. However, he had overlooked the fact that the last item discussed at the meeting had been the managers' concern about personnel and also that some people cannot think of needs in any terms but dollars.

In this communication situation, different fields of reference led to the misunderstanding. Both sender and receiver each had a "clear picture" in his head about what the message meant, but neither checked with the other to see if the pictures were the same. The failure of the managers to feed back what they "understood" and the failure on the part of the district manager to elicit feedback seriously interfered with the communication and the operation of the organization.

What Is Feedback?

The term feedback has become an administrative cliché, not only overworked but also used to mean a large variety of different concepts. As is true with almost any word, people associate many different meanings with it. The term feedback evolved out of applications of cybernetic principles in electromechanical processes. Climbing down the abstraction ladder, we translate that last sentence to mean: feedback is a process by which a system corrects its own behavior or performance. And a system, in the communication sense, can mean a person.

Although the term is relatively new, it is an old idea. An elementary example of feedback is the windmill that at one time was used extensively on the farms in this country. For the windmill to function properly, it must face into the wind. To accomplish this, the windmill has a tail devised so that the mechanism continually corrects itself to face into the prevailing winds. This simple device is actually a feedback mechanism because it corrects its own function.

Another simple example is the automatic control of furnaces that we use in our businesses and homes. Thermostats feed information about the furnace's output back into the system, and the energy source is then modified to maintain the desired temperature. Feedback can be described, then, as a self-governing, goal-seeking system which is capable of scanning its own performance and comparing it with its intended or actual performance. The data are then used to guide or change future actions.

In face-to-face communication, almost continuous feedback is possible and desirable. Whether speaking to one or to a group, you can never know enough about the moment-to-moment reaction of your audience. The effective communicator must become sensitive to all clues that indicate how his or her listeners are reacting. If you are continually monitoring the receiver's reaction, you can modify your message. Even your intent, or what you thought you could accomplish, may need to be revised according to the feedback you receive.

So far we have been concerned primarily with what is known as external feedback; that is, information you receive. There is another dimension, however, which is known as internal feedback. Internal feedback is in operation when you begin to reflect about something you have just said and realize that it does not sound correct or clear. You may say something like, "Well, that wasn't what I meant," or, "That didn't sound right," or "Let me put that another way." Of course, these two types of feedback are at work simultaneously and each often affects the other. An effective communicator is also an effective listener to what he himself has to say. By listening to his own messages he may decide it is desirable to change or alter what he has said.

When we speak to another person we expect a response. This anticipation results from internal feedback that causes us to expect a certain behavior to occur. Internal feedback is at work when we correct what we intend to say before we say it, on the basis of what we think will be the response of the listener.

Feedback can also be positive or negative in nature. Perhaps unconsciously, the receiver is using feedback as a device to modify behavior. For example, the response of an audience to a speaker can greatly modify the speaker's behavior. Applause or nods of agreement, can encourage the speaker to continue the type of communication in which he or she is engaging. On the other hand, responses such as boos, inattention, yawns, or frowns, will cause the speaker, if sensitive to this behavior, to modify his or her communication to be more in line with the expectation of the audience. This is one reason why it can be said that the audience really controls the speaker. Whether we like it or not we are more the servants of our listeners than their masters.

Although feedback is necessary to achieve effective communication it can also be very troublesome. People frequently say that they want feedback, but then do nothing to encourage, receive, or interpret it. We wonder if such people really want feedback and if they have the personal security to accept constructive suggestions.

Another troublesome feature is that feedback is time-consuming. We have had managers tell us that they simply did not have time for feedback—that it took too much time and they had a business to run. So they tell their staffs what they expect of them and that is that. We certainly can understand their frustration. But we sometimes ask, "Can you afford the risk that comes from the lack of feedback?" True, communication without feedback is faster. What's more, there are certain times when such one-way communication is necessary and effective. But communication without feedback is far less likely to be as accurate as communication with feedback.

In training seminars we use an exercise to illustrate this phenomenon. We have a simple puzzle that we ask participants to assemble. In the first part of the activity, we have one individual explain to another how to assemble the puzzle, and he or she does so without any feedback from the receiver. It is one-way communication, with one person giving directions to the other. The time required to make the explanation usually runs from two to seven minutes. We have repeated this game well over a hundred times and have yet to have the puzzle correctly assembled when instructions are given without feedback.

In the second half of the exercise, the same situation is used except that the participants can talk freely. They may ask questions, volunteer information, do whatever they wish except, of course, look at the solution to the puzzle. The time consumed, with feedback, can run to as much as 45 minutes, but in almost every case, the individuals have been able to assemble the puzzle correctly. It is often very surprising to the participants how much longer it takes when they are giving instruction with feedback, but they are also very impressed with how much more accurate the results are.

Occasionally, we find that the receiving of feedback can be emotionally disturbing. As we have carried out this puzzle experiment, we have found that some individuals have experienced a great deal of frustration from the kind of feedback they have received. People do not like to have their mistakes and oversights exposed. In attempting to assemble the puzzle, receivers sometimes make uncomplimentary remarks about the sender's intelligence and skills. On a few occasions we have seen participants become visibly angry.

From honest feedback you may learn that people do not think as highly of you as you thought they did, or that your style of management is not as effective as you think it is. However, if you're really concerned about the effectiveness of your communication, this knowledge can help alter your communicative behavior for the better.

Feedback comes in a variety of forms. It can be verbal or nonverbal, direct or indirect, immediate or delayed. In the following paragraphs, two types of response will be investigated.

Behavior as a Response

How the other person acts or responds to our communication gives us important clues about the effectiveness of our message. A good example is the response you receive from directions you give. In Chapter One, we used the illustration of a manager asking an employee to clean up a mess. The manager later observed that Walt was performing the requested task and therefore judged the communication to be effective.

However, this is probably the poorest form of feedback since it is received "after the act" and can serve only to modify future communication. It does not serve as a corrective device for the current interaction. Responses of this nature are delayed and indirect and therefore, less useful. There are occasions when this type of feedback is all that is available, however. When this is true the sender should be willing to look back at the communicative act, and evaluate it so that in the future he or she can send a more effective message.

In this type of response it is more difficult to analyze and locate possible problems. In the case of the instructions to Walt, if the manager had found Walt was doing something else and the mess had not been cleaned, what would be his reaction? If he is like most of us, he would wonder what was wrong with Walt, not what is wrong with himself or his communication. When our directions are not carried out it is easy for us to assume the fault lies with the other person. How could it be our fault? The message was clear and Walt said he understood and would do as requested. Maybe so, and maybe not. The point is that when a situation like this occurs, rarely does the sender stop and say, "What happened?" The tendency is to blame, not investigate. Yet only through investigation can we learn the "why." When this answer is found, the message may need to be "corrected."

Paraphrasing as Feedback

One of the causes of breakdown in communication is the failure of the parties in the communicative act to provide adequate checking of what the other one meant. To avoid such breakdowns, an effective technique is to paraphrase what you understand each other to be saying. The receiver restates or paraphrases the message to see if he has heard or perceived the intended meaning of the communication. This doesn't mean to parrot back exactly what was said, but rather to put the message in your own words. It doesn't take understanding to parrot—only a good memory. Paraphrasing provides the sender an opportunity to discover if the message he sent was adequately received. Responses of this type often begin in the following fashion: "What I think you are saying is. . . ." Then the speaker continues to paraphrase what he thinks the speaker said. If the paraphrase is not adequate or accurate the sender can then make the necessary changes.

Don't expect meaningful corrective communication in asking, "What do you mean?" Such a question does not tell the sender enough for him to make adequate corrections. Generally, he simply repeats what he said before, which is of little help if the receiver does not understand. If the receiver feeds back in paraphrase what he thinks was said, errors in his perception can be pinpointed more quickly and more effectively.

In seeking feedback, the sender often asks the question "Do you understand?" This is probably the poorest way of securing adequate feedback. When one is asked if he understands, especially from someone of higher status, he is most likely to respond in the affirmative. Certainly we have put all of the pressure upon him to respond that way. Of course, he understands what he thinks he understands, and even if he doesn't he is reluctant to appear stupid. A far better way of getting good feedback is to ask *what* he understands. This gives the receiver the opportunity to state his perceptions and reveal gaps or misconceptions in what he has grasped.

The next time you are in an argument with someone, try the paraphrase technique. Before you unleash your rebuttal, do your best to state fairly the other person's viewpoint. This will do two things. First, it will surprise him that you have really been listening to his side of the controversy, and it may cause him to be less on the defensive and to try listening better to you. Second, it gives the individual an opportunity to say, "No, that's not quite what I meant . . .," and you may be on the way to clarifying the issue and making it easier for both of you to deal with it.

Barriers to Feedback

Your subordinates have a way of discovering what you like to hear, and they often can be very proficient in tailoring messages to meet your expectations. If you will tolerate only good news, for example, the subordinates will tend, almost exclusively, to provide you with happy tidings. If such a climate exists and the subordinates tell you only what you want to hear, then you are deprived of the realities with which you are expected to deal. This has caused many managers to operate in what they thought was an ideal situation only to discover that the whole organization was crumbling around them. When the structure collapses, these managers can't understand how it could have happened to them when everything was apparently going so well.

Managers need to be fully aware of the ever-dynamic and ever-changing environment of their organizations. Change is a part of everyday life. The competent manager must create a climate which helps the staff adjust to change. Subordinates must be sure that if they volunteer critical feedback they will be encouraged, not punished.

Frequently, status becomes a barrier to effective feedback. Whenever someone with high status within an organization sends a message down through the system, it can be distorted as it passes from person to person. If an individual is message-centered to the extent that he places a literal interpretation upon the words received, rather than seeking to find out what the sender meant, he may have gross misconceptions about intention. Such people may hear overtones of deeper meanings that were not intended. Of course, a person with lesser status is often very concerned about the personal relationship with the superior who has control over him. He may wonder if the manager likes him, whether he is satisfied with his work, or whether he will be punished or rewarded.

As a manager you have a supervisory relationship with a number of people. You attention is therefore scattered throughout your span of command. It is certainly not uncommon for you to view each individual relationship as less important than the whole, because you supervise a lot of people. And you are just as likely to assume that the subordinates will view the relationship in the same fashion as you do. This can be a hazardous assumption. Managers frequently search for feedback only on the basis of the importance of the message to them and to their whole organization rather than its importance to the subordinates. When this occurs the manager becomes a source-centered communicator, one who is more concerned with the message sent than with the message received. Such an individual fails to pick up cues indicating potential trouble.

As a manager you must always be on guard that you do not communicate to your subordinates, either verbally or nonverbally, that you regard yourself as a person who is concerned only with setting objectives and reviewing performance. If you communicate that you feel you do not have the responsibility to clarify the nature of a job or to aid in the solution of a problem or just to be helpful, you have erected a barrier against feedback. If your subordinates see you as a leader who feels, "My job is to tell you what to do and how well you have done it," you can be sure they will hesitate to give you feedback on the work situation.

Prematurely evaluating the messages you do hear is another barrier. Your first job is to make certain that you have received the message and fully understand it. Then and only then can you adequately judge a message. When you receive negative feedback, all the pressure is on you to respond in a threatening or defensive tone. But such a response is likely to block communication and increase hostile feelings. When such a climate develops, meaningful feedback ceases.

Forcing feedback upon someone is another barrier. If you give feedback to an individual and he does not alter his response or behavior, it rarely enhances the communication to continue providing feedback. If your feedback has been rejected, you may not be helping by repeating it. This kind of behavior should provide feedback to you that something is wrong with the relationship, and your attention should be focused on improving the relationship. If a person is unable to deal with feedback, it is unwise to insist that he or she receive it.

How to Get Feedback

There is too little systematic use of feedback in most of our interpersonal relations. Since communication has not been regarded as a skill which one improves, it is not uncommon to find that communication patterns have developed which ignore the possibilities and usefulness of feedback.

Two dimensions of feedback are of concern to effective communicators. First, as senders, we are required to be sensitive to feedback from our receivers; and second, we, as receivers of messages, must be willing to test what we receive by checking with the sender as to the meaning, intent, purpose, and function. If more meaningful feedback can be developed between people, there could be a generally higher level of understanding and more effective development of human interaction.

These are worthy goals, but how do we develop the skill of getting and using feedback? The following are some ways:

1. **Actively seek feedback.** You must take an active role in encouraging people to speak up and raise questions—even to disagree. You must take the time to respond to questions and to point out their necessity in maintaining effective interaction. Nonverbal elements of communications are of crucial importance in communicating to subordinates that you are sincere in your interest in feedback.

2. **Provide time for feedback.** Don't assume that feedback will happen just because you have said you desire it. In many organizations it seems to work best if specific times are set for feedback sessions. Holding regular sessions is better than waiting until the problems accumulate and become magnified.

One corporation achieved successful feedback by setting up special tables in the cafeteria and arranging for three employees at a time to have lunch with a supervisor other than their own. Managers were briefed on how to listen more effectively and were required to prepare a written report daily of the units the employees came from (not their names) and the problem areas that were identified. Not only did management gain a much better understanding of how the rank-and-file employee felt, but they were also able to correct some situations immediately, thus greatly improving morale.[1]

3. Plan ahead for feedback sessions. Give some thought to the best way to elicit honest feedback. What's going on that can be used as a springboard for discussion? Little is gained from casual, offhand questions like, "Well, does anybody have anything to say?" or "Anybody have any problems they want to talk about?" or "Is everything going all right?"

4. Encourage feedback by giving it yourself. As a manager you can provide a model of giving feedback constructively and tactfully. By providing occasions for dialogues, discussions, and real give-and-take, you can make sure your ideas and instructions are not dispensed in a one-way fashion.

5. Use silence to encourage feedback. If you really want the other person to feed back data to you, you must be willing to remain silent long enough for him or her to do so. With pressures and tensions on you, there is a strong tendency to become impatient with an employee who is slow to respond. But, unless you are willing to wait—without feeling that you have to fill the silence—you may not get the feedback you need. What seems like a long period of time to you may seem very brief to a subordinate who is trying to collect and organize his or her thoughts. Here again, watch your nonverbal behavior while you are waiting. If you communicate impatience or criticism, your silence is of negative rather than positive value.

6. Be alert to nonverbal feedback. In Chapter Four we discussed the difficulty of censoring our own nonverbal behavior. We pointed out that frequently the honest or true message is inadvertently transmitted through nonverbal actions or tones of voice. An effective

1. J.N. Smith, "Operation Speakeasy: An Experiment in Communication," *Management Review,* Vol. 62 (March, 1973).

manager is continually watching for the slightest indication in the behavior of his or her subordinates that the message is not clear or is inconsistent, or that there is some problem associated with the communication. For example, as you are giving instructions, a subordinate tells you that he understands, but at the same time he is wearing a frown or puzzled look. It is far better, in this case, to trust the nonverbal message you receive rather than the verbal one.

7. **Use questions for clarification.** Questions can help determine if we have the same definitions or meanings for words. For example, what do you mean by "unsatisfactory"? What do you mean by "full responsibility," "he lacks motivation," or "he is only so-so"? The list is endless, but as we pointed out earlier, people have a wide difference of meanings for the same words, and asking questions can both elicit feedback and create shared meanings.

8. **Reward feedback.** This is easy to do when the feedback we receive is positive; it is very difficult when it is negative. However, both positive and negative feedback are necessary for you to know and understand the realities of your organization and the people involved. The rewards do not necessarily have to be of great significance, but they should be enough to make the individual feel that it was worth his time. Often a simple, sincerely meant "thank you" is sufficient. If the situation dictates, a written note expressing your appreciation is also an effective reward. If someone has made an unusually significant contribution, you may wish to write a more formal letter and forward a copy to the next higher level of management.

The Analysis and Application of Feedback

The following three sample situations provide material for analysis and critique on giving and receiving feedback.

Situation 1

Bob: Can I speak with you a moment?

Manager: Certainly, Bob. Come in and sit down.

Bob: I thought I'd like to talk to you about getting that promotion.

Manager: Well, I understand how you feel about this, Bob.

Bob:	How could you? You are not in a position. . . .
Manager:	Well, of course not. But I understand how disappointed you must be.
Bob:	Yes, that's right.
Manager:	In making that promotion, we based it entirely upon performance, and it had nothing to do with seniority. I'm sure you'll agree that Vernon had a better record, so we just simply had to select him over you. Now let me tell you what I'd do if I were in your position. I'd upgrade my skills so that the next time there's a promotion, you will be in a better position to get it. Now doesn't that make sense?
Bob:	Well, I guess so, but. . . .
Manager:	Good. I'm glad you agree with me. We'll have a chance to talk about this later when things slack off a bit. Right now I'm just buried in work, so if you'll excuse me. . . .

How effective was the feedback in this situation? Did the manager do all that he could to make certain that he read Bob's feedback? Do you feel as sure as the manager seems to be that Bob agrees with his assessment of the situation? Do you regard the feedback as adequate or inadequate, and why?

As you reread the conversation, you will note that the manager did not receive enough feedback. The "I guess so, but . . ." can only be regarded as a very weak agreement, and the response seemed more forced by the status of the manager than by real agreement on the part of the employee. Besides, Bob was interrupted so that the manager will never know what reservations he was about to share. There seems to be no question about Bob's understanding the manager's position, but did the manager understand Bob's? We can say the feedback was insufficient and inadequate because it failed to clarify the feeling and attitude of the employee. Better feedback could have been gained if the manager had asked an open-ended question, such as, "How can I help you improve your skills?" or "What can we do to help you continue your self-development?" In addition, it would have helped if the manager had done more listening and less talking.

Let's not forget the feedback the manager gave. It would have been much better if he had set a definite time if, in fact, he was too busy then to talk to Bob. It is not very likely that the employee left the manager's office feeling very secure about his work situation. How motivated to upgrade his skills do you think Bob will be?

Situation 2

Suppose you receive the following request from your supervisor: "The report you handed in last week had a number of errors in it, and we need to discuss it. Let's get together Monday in my office at 4 p.m."

Since this is a simple message and a clear-cut request to be in a certain place at a specific time, would you say there was no need for feedback? Would you say this message itself implies that the receiver may provide feedback? Or would you say that this message offered very little opportunity for feedback?

Our feeling is that this kind of message leaves little room for feedback. What's more, the circumstances do not encourage feedback from the subordinate. It would be very easy for the subordinate to read his own meanings into the message. Is strong criticism implied or mere disapproval? Are the errors insignificant, or are they serious? Should the subordinate bring any records or materials with him when he appears at the meeting? Without an opportunity to clarify some of these aspects, what kind of condition do you expect the subordinate to be in by Monday afternoon?

Situation 3

Manager:	Ted, I'd like to ask you a few questions about our new billing system.
Ted:	Sure, shoot.
Manager:	Well, my first question concerns the new system as compared to the old one. Do you think the new system is better?
Ted:	Oh, sure, definitely. It's a big improvement.
Manager:	I'm sure glad of that. Have you had any problems with it?
Ted:	Oh, a few so far. But we found the errors without much trouble.
Manager:	Then the people are happy with it, aren't they?
Ted:	I think so. Don and Paul have been complaining about a few things, but the program is sound.
Manager:	Great. I'm glad everything is going so well. Appreciate your help, Ted. Keep me posted.
Ted:	Sure will. See yah.

As you look at this interaction, how do you evaluate it? Would you say this was successful communication? Did the manager get the answers he needed? Or did you see it largely as unproductive? How effective were the questions asked by the manager? Which of the following statements best describes the key to the problem? (1) There wasn't enough feedback from Ted. (2) There wasn't enough feedback from the manager. (3) There wasn't enough feedback from either one.

This particular example has all the appearance of effective communication. Remember, however, for feedback to be effective, it must flow both ways. In this case there was not enough feedback in either direction. Part of the blame can be placed on the manager because he has the responsibility to get and give feedback. It is easy to fault Ted and say that he failed to provide the manager with essential information, yet the manager received several clues to possible difficulties and did nothing to follow up on them. When his initial questions did not get good feedback, he should have asked questions such as, "Where are the breakdowns?" and "What is the nature of the complaints?" These kinds of questions would have required Ted to respond in a more definite manner. By probing Ted's superficial comments, the manager could have elicited the data necessary to make proper judgments even though Ted may not have analyzed the situation accurately or is withholding information to avoid upsetting the boss.

"Who Is to Blame?"

In this chapter we have been concerned with the role feedback plays in producing understanding between people. We have contended that if there is open and free feedback within an organization, the manager will have a better perception of reality. When communication breaks down, the inept manager most likely asks, "Who is to blame?" Rarely does he consider himself a potential part of the problem. A more sophisticated manager will ask, instead, "How can we correct the situation that exists and move ahead?"

Edward Harwell recounts the following incident in one store:

An unusual situation occurred in [a] store where the new manager seemed thoroughly unable to keep any cashiers. Almost every new cashier would stay a few weeks, then quit, and when the manager interviewed them, the reasons were always the same: a better job, dissatisfaction with the work, the hours, the pay, and so forth. After several months, the supervisor persuaded the company that the manager simply could not handle people and the manager was fired.

One of the cashiers finally revealed the real reason for this epidemic of resignations. It seemed that a regular cashier, who had been hired by the store about the same time as the released manager had taken over, was addicted to narcotics and continually solicited loans from other cashiers, which were never repaid. Though the employee had a pleasant personality and got along well with co-workers, the cashier's habit and financial problems put the other employees on the spot. Rather than complain to management, they quit.[2]

In this incident it was easy enough to put the blame on the manager. All too frequently managers are blamed, but actually they are not trained in the effective use of feedback in their communication systems. The cashiers in the above example were confronted with three alternatives: first, they could continue their jobs and tolerate the addicted cashier; second, they could tell the manager about the problem so that he could take some action; or finally, they could leave their jobs.

The fact that they chose the most severe alternative indicates that the climate did not encourage or tolerate open communication. If there had been open and free communication in the first place, enhanced by adequate feedback, this situation would have been readily diagnosed; and much of the heartbreak experienced by the people involved would have been avoided.

Effective managers *must* fulfill their responsibility both to get and to give feedback.

---

2. Edward M. Harwell, *Personnel Management and Training*, p. 185.

6

Sharpening Communication Skills

In Chapter One we pointed out that communication means a lot more than the simple flow of information. We observed that thinking was the foundation of communication since any purposeful communication starts with a thought or idea. Two wings can be built on this foundation: one we call transmitting skills, speaking and writing, and the other we label receiving skills, reading and listening. Nonverbal behavior is considered a function of both transmitting and receiving. In this chapter we will analyze the individual communication skills in greater depth.

Thinking: The Foundation of Communication

This section deals with a subject which has fascinated people for centuries—the human mind. This fascination has resulted in untold numbers of volumes concerning the nature of thinking. It is not our intention either to add to the stacks of tomes on this subject or to attempt to provide "instant information." We will, however, highlight some of the essentials that are the most useful in everyday communication.

One of the marks of effective managers is their ability to think critically. The process of thinking results in a commitment. That's right—a commitment, or a personal resolution to do, or to cease from doing some act; to adopt or to reject some opinion; to anticipate doing something; or to adopt or to reject some objective.

Now, let's look at the two major kinds of thinking: intrapersonal (inside our own heads) and interpersonal (in association with other people).

Intrapersonal Thinking

Intrapersonal thinking involves those commitments we make internally and which are not shared with anyone else. Some of the decisions we make this way include such matters as what we are going to say at a given moment, the selection of people to talk with, the purpose of our talking, and commitments we make by ourselves without direct reference to anyone else.

One of the areas of intrapersonal thinking is the process of feedback. Out of all the feedback we receive, we select the signals that are most useful; then we decide on the meaning of those signals. The very creation of meaning by an individual is done through intrapersonal thinking.

As a food store manager walks through the produce department one morning, he notices several overripe apples. Removing them, he thinks, "Tom is letting down on his work. I'm going to have to call him in and talk to him again." When the manager gets to the front of the store, he finds that there are no shopping carts available for the customers. He goes to the microphone and requests that carts be gathered in from the parking lot. He is irritated by this seeming lack of concern by the stockers whose responsibility it is to see that the shopping carts are brought in. Wondering what is the matter with young people today, he concludes, "Oh well, what can you expect nowadays?"

In this illustration, the manager engaged in intrapersonal thinking. Although the decisions he reached and the observations he made eventually would have direct bearing on other people, the process of the thinking was not shared or communicated verbally.

Interpersonal Thinking

Interpersonal thinking, as the term implies, involves other people more directly. When any two people sit down to talk together, they quickly become involved in deciding what they will talk about. They make some kind of commitment as to how they are going to relate to each other.

When you become involved in a group, whether it is an agenda-packed staff meeting or an informal gathering, one of the decisions you must make (and generally it is done unconsciously) has to do with the amount of control you will allow others to have over you and your actions.

You must also determine to what extent you will allow others to have an effect on your thinking process. Although we are seldom aware of the process of making this decision, each time we associate with another person we confront the issue of control. Our thinking process permits us to make decisions so rapidly we are often unaware that the process is going on.

What Is Involved in Effective Thinking?

Whether our thinking is done intrapersonally or interpersonally, it results in what we commonly call ideas. These ideas are the substance of what we seek to transmit when we communicate.

The quality of thinking depends on how well informed we are and how well we can select and use information. But even if we make a decision based on the available facts it won't necessarily be the "right" decision. Being human, we sometimes have to make decisions based on incomplete data. Sometimes we draw the wrong conclusion. For example, a person may weigh all the facts he or she can get before accepting a new job, only to find later that there is a personality conflict with the new boss which outweighs all the positive factors.

It is also possible for us to possess many facts in one area but few in others. We may make the mistake of assuming a person is an expert in all fields; yet we know that a competent lawyer may be a novice in solving medical problems, and a competent mechanic may be quite ineffective at solving problems in human relations.

If the correctness of a decision is not a measure of the effectiveness of our thinking, just what are the indicators then? Two key

aspects of effective thinking are reality-testing and probability-estimating.

Reality-testing is the process of checking out what is real—what
is consistent with the "real world" around us. It involves separating
out fact from fancy, traditions, opinions, and archaic feelings. It
includes perceiving and evaluating the current situation and relating
the data to past knowledge and experience. Reality-testing, in essence,
permits us to select alternative solutions.

The process of probability-estimating occurs when we have alternative solutions with which to deal. We can then estimate the
probable consequences of the various courses of action open to us.
We take a critical look at each possible solution and determine which
is the most desirable course of action to follow. Just as there are
certain odds involved in flipping a coin or betting at the race track,
there are also odds or probabilities of successful decision-making
when we choose among available alternatives.

Critical, effective thinking is based on objective appraisals of the
situation and thought processes that are communicated in a straightforward, unemotional manner. Consider an example: A manager has
been attempting to explain a new procedure to an employee. It is
obvious that the subordinate doesn't like the new system, and he
finally says something like this: "Boy, I'll tell you, I never cease to
be amazed by the way a little bit of power goes to the heads of some
people! I swear, you managers are all alike."

There are several possible ways in which the manager could react
to this. Here are three possible responses. Which one seems to be the
result of the most effective thinking?

Response A: You're not implying that power has gone to my
head, are you? If you can't take what I say at face
value then that's your problem.

Response B: Now just a minute! Who do you think you are? Who
do you think you're talking to? You not only question my integrity but my authority as a manager as
well.

Response C: Well, it's apparent you have strong feelings about
something, but I'm not sure about what. Maybe this
would be a good time for you to level with me,
okay?

It should be apparent that responses A and B are the results of
ineffective thinking. Both appear to be based on archaic data devoid
of any reality-testing or probability-estimating. Response A seems to

be the product of a thinking process which relies more on feeling than logic and is more concerned with maintaining position and authority than in clarifying communication. Response B reveals an acute concern for maintaining the manager's self-concept of high power and authority. The manager seems to be more concerned with sending a message about himself than about the topic under discussion.

Response C is less emotional and is concerned with determining the facts in the situation and looking for an avenue for mediation. The focus of this response is solving the problem rather than merely maintaining status. The manager has engaged in effective thinking in Response C.

In this brief introduction to effective thinking, we have suggested the importance of weighing the alternatives we find at our choice points, as well as checking out the potential effects. In Chapter Nine we will look more extensively at the process of reasoning when we discuss decision-making and problem-solving from other perspectives.

Transmitting Skills: Speaking and Writing

Before we begin our examination of these skills individually, let's review the amount of time a manager spends on them in his or her work.

One of the first attempts to measure the time managers and other professionals use in communicating was made by Paul Rankin in 1929. He studied a cross section of executives from all types of businesses and professions and found that the average manager spends approximately 70 percent of his or her day communicating. However, Rankin's most startling discovery was that managers spend the greatest amount of time doing the things for which their education had prepared them the least. The survey showed that 45 percent of a manager's communication time is spent in listening, 30 percent in speaking, 16 percent in reading, and only 9 percent in writing. Most subjects had been taught to read and write; few had received any instruction in speaking or listening.

A more recent survey reveals almost identical data. Reporting in the June, 1962, issue of the *Journal of Communication,* E.T. Klemmer and F.W. Snyder found that managers spend approximately 89 percent of their time in some form of communication activity. They also found that managers' communication time is divided in the following fashion: 20 percent devoted to writing, 17 percent to reading, and 63 percent to talking and listening. It should be noted that this sample was made at a large communication research and development laboratory, which possibly explains the relatively high percentages of writing and reading, certainly not typical of managers in most businesses. Another difficulty with the data is that the researchers did not attempt to separate the time spent in face-to-face speaking from that of listening.

The Skill of Speaking

Speech and the physical process of speaking are complicated. We are not referring to the complexities of originating ideas and encoding them into language; we are referring specifically to the highly complex process of producing sounds.

One reason for this complexity is that there is no single speech organ. The eyes see, the ears hear; but which organ speaks? Not the tongue, the lungs, the larynx, nor the brain—although all of these are involved. Speech is not a primary function of our organs; it has been superimposed by painstaking development. We use our throats to speak, but their more vital function is to swallow; we use our lungs to supply us with air for speaking, but providing us with air for breathing is more important. When we see deaf children struggling to produce sounds they cannot hear, we recognize the fundamental role the ear plays in speech; yet the ear's primary function is to hear. Our ability to speak, then, is learned, not inherited, and in order to speak we must use a variety of organs which were primarily designed for other functions.

By its very nature, speech is highly transitory. For the most part, words once spoken are lost forever except as they can be replicated in the minds of those who were present when the words were uttered, or unless they are captured on tape. Moreover, there is no completely accurate way for writing to reproduce speech. Even a verbatim transcript of a speech lacks the nuances of vocal variations and nonverbal behavior.

Another area for skill development is in the creation and construction of messages themselves. To do this effectively we must know what results we want from our effort to communicate. Unless we have a clear purpose in mind we won't know how best to select and organize our ideas. What's more, we won't be able to evaluate our success. Another often overlooked consideration is that the oral presentation of ideas must also meet the needs of the listener. If our speech is not adapted to the listener's needs and interests, we are merely talking to ourselves.

The Skill of Writing

Throughout this book we have talked about the significant role of oral communication. We have said that speaking dominates a large portion of our communicative endeavors. However, a sending skill that is often undervalued is that of writing.

In training programs we frequently ask participants about the role writing plays in their particular jobs. When we ask what kind of writing they do, the response is often "only what we have to do." Very few say that they like to write. Apparently we are all born non-writers and most of us would just as soon stay that way. For many, writing has always been an unpleasant chore. Even answering a simple letter can be a traumatic experience.

One reason we seem to fear writing is that it has a permanent quality and is there for others to look at. If we make a grammatical mistake or our words come out in awkward clumps, there it is on paper for people to see and judge us by. We become much more self-conscious about writing and have a tendency to be flowery or formal. Perhaps the fear and distaste of writing can be blamed on our teachers who drilled us in boring rules and criticized us for our writing mistakes far more than for mistakes in verbal language. Today, when we sit down to write a letter or a report, many of us are still trying to please an elementary school teacher or get good grades on a composition. We are not writing a letter to the addressee or making a report to the vice president; we are trying to write a composition.

Another reason that writing seems so difficult is that it has the reputation of an art (which of course it is) that depends on inspiration (which of course it doesn't). Writing is a craft that requires effort more than inspiration. No one is inherently more talented than any other person when it comes to writing in ways that can be easily understood.

Although this desire to avoid all writing seems a common condition of many of us, research indicates that, like it or not, we must spend approximately 10 percent of our communication time in writing. Instead of simply doing it as we have always done, we could take the time to evaluate our writing and try to find ways to make it more meaningful and interesting.

A class in advertising writing used as its main theme the slogan, *"Remember, they don't want to read it!"* If we keep in mind how many pieces of paper flood onto our desks, and that busy people really "don't want to read" what we have written, we will probably do a better job of capturing the reader's attention. We should tell readers quickly why they should read what we have written, and we should make clear what we want them to do, think, or feel as a result of what we write.

Comparing the Transmitting Skills

Excluding the unfortunate people who have handicaps, everyone in the world has the capacity to learn to speak. Even the most remote jungle tribes have primitive spoken languages. However, not all cultures have written languages. It is still true today that considerably less than half the population of the world can read and write any language.

Learning to talk is an inevitable and natural part of the human environment. We could not help but learn to speak, and we did so without conscious effort. In a sense we were not taught to speak; we learned from being spoken to. Writing, however, requires a more or less formal teaching situation. Most of us have no recollection of learning to speak, but we have a clear memory of the trauma of trying to learn to write.

People consciously surrounded by the spoken word, such as travelers in foreign countries, eventually will come to understand the strange language, if only a little, and learn to speak it slightly. However, an individual can be surrounded all of his life by the written word without ever being able to reproduce it. Learning to read and write requires conscious effort. We must learn the marks and the connections between the written marks and the sounds they make. On one hand we can say that learning to speak is unavoidable; on the other hand, learning to write is altogether too avoidable.

Have you ever heard of anyone writing in his sleep? Thinking is frequently described as talking to oneself, but have you ever heard it described as writing to oneself? These observations suggest a more intimate connection between speech and the thought process than there is between writing and the thought process. Writing lacks the spontaneity of speech. In general, when we want to say something, we just say it. But when we want to write something, we need tools and a plan and minimum distractions.

Some people, when asked to give a speech or an oral presentation of any kind, are only comfortable if they write it all out first. They fear a memory lapse or stage fright and need the security of a written message. What happens in this case, however, is that we have an essay on its hind legs that is an oral reading rather than an oral speech. The material lacks the true spontaneity of speech and therefore lacks the directness that helps keep the listeners' attention.

Some Essentials for Adequate Transmitting

1. The first essential for adequate speaking or writing is the ability to think clearly. In the first part of this chapter we discussed the role of thinking in the process of communication. We suggested that unless we can think adequately, none of the skills of communication can be maximized. Unless we are effective thinkers, all our concern with techniques is futile. Does the following appear to have been clearly thought through? "This is—uh—a good time to begin—uh—you know—thinking about—I mean preparing for—the—uh—Christmas season."

2. The second essential is simply having something to say. Effective communication does not exist in isolation. We must have a concern about what is to be communicated and to whom it is sent. Few people can speak or write well about something which is of no importance or significance to them or to their receivers. We are all familiar with the hackneyed flattery that we hear from some speakers. How concerned is the speaker who begins with this cliché? "I'm glad to see so many young people here tonight. Your bright and eager faces remind us that the youth of today are the leaders of tomorrow. And your presence here is a high tribute to your parents, whose devotion and self-sacrifice . . ."

3. Another essential is having a specific purpose. To be effective, a purpose must be stated in terms of the receiver's needs, not in terms of the sender's. "What does the other person need or want to know?" This is a more important question than "What do I want to tell him?" If our purpose is merely to "write a letter" or "make a speech," the net result can never be measured in any functional way. To write or speak well, we must decide ahead of time what result we want and expect to get from the receiver.

4. The fourth essential is the possession of thorough knowledge of the subject. For instance, during a staff meeting, one of the department heads is asked about security in his department. "Well, I don't know too much about it," he begins. "This really isn't my area you know, and I'm afraid you all know more about it than I do, but I guess it wouldn't hurt to take a look at it again." It is not likely, by the time he finishes his statement, that the receivers of this message are waiting with any degree of anticipation for enlightened information. Not only must a writer or speaker know the subject; he or she must also have an understanding of the communication process which, in turn, rests upon an adequate knowledge of the qualities, functions, tools, and techniques of communication.

5. The last point, but the most important, is the ability to put oneself in the place of the receiver. It is asking yourself what it is like to "live" in the other person's world. What does he or she need to know to clarify understanding? This ability to be empathetic—to walk in another's shoes—can be acquired, but it takes conscious effort. Henry Ford once said that the secret of success in any endeavor is to see the person's problem from the other viewpoint.

Improving Transmitting Skills

Let's take a closer look at writing. For many people the most difficult part of writing is getting the point of the pencil on the sheet of paper or striking the first key on the typewriter to make a mark on that big piece of blank paper. The answer is simply to get started—to get something down on paper. If we approach that blank sheet of paper with the attitude that it will not be material that is carved in stone, and that we can change it and improve upon it later, the blank sheet of paper is less threatening. Do not wait until you can write the perfect sentence or the perfect paragraph, or for witty phrases, or for a burst of brilliance. Do not be surprised or disappointed if you fail to demonstrate lofty qualities in your first draft. Getting started is the important thing.

Evaluating what we have written is the next step. We need to cultivate a detached air and pretend we are reading the work of a stranger. We need to be critical and willing to change. The very least we should do is allow sufficient time to proofread what we have written. The best thing to do, if at all possible, is to put what we have written away and let it simmer for a day or so and then take another look. Those lines which seem to be truly inspired at 1 a.m. may not seem quite so stirring when read in the cold light of day. In other words, a good writer is also a good rewriter.

An effective writer also must overcome the "Inadequate Vocabulary Syndrome." Managers are frequently reluctant to write because they believe their vocabularies are too limited. However, few people have a vocabulary so limited that it would severely limit their writing ability. Maybe this is an excuse to avoid writing.

We need to be aware of the fact that the written language is quite different from the spoken language. Can you imagine yourself saying the following to a customer who has complained about service? "In reply to your recent communication, please be advised that an investigation was conducted which revealed that our long-standing rules were, in fact, violated. We wish to assure you that the matter has been corrected and the situation you referred to in your letter will not occur in the future."

Our written language is inevitably more formal than our spoken language. We can be forgiven for incomplete sentences or thoughts when we speak, but not when we write. We need to adjust our oral and written languages to what is most meaningful to our readers and listeners. This does not mean we are talking down; it means we are adjusting to our receiver's needs.

We cannot emphasize too much that we write and speak to achieve a specific purpose. If we are achieving our purpose consistently, we are successful. If we are not, then we will not be successful. The ultimate criterion exists not in the written or spoken product itself, but rather in the reader's or listener's reaction to it.

Receiving Skills: Reading and Listening

Now let's take a look at the receiving skills. Much too frequently, we believe, communication training focuses primarily on the sending skills. However, unless the message is received, communication does not occur.

The Reading Skill

There is a great deal of interest today in learning to read faster. This concern may reflect the fact that we all have more and more material that we are expected to read. There simply isn't enough time to read carefully everything we receive.

Most of us began learning to read in kindergarten or the first grade, at approximately the age of five or six. Like learning to write, learning to read does not come naturally. A conscious effort must be made, and we must be taught by someone.

Have you ever made a mental note of how many written messages there are for the public? What about those for employees? We made a survey of one business and found more than 250 written messages. There were necessary messages providing information, giving directions, and calling attention to various regulations; and this list does not even include all the written messages on the various items for sale. But did you ever consider how many items there are in an organization which have writing on them? Certainly you are surrounded by much more writing than your predecessors were.

People differ widely in their reading ability. The range is much broader than that which exists in speaking or in understanding speech. One difference is the rate or speed with which we read. One person may read a book in three hours while another may take 20 or more. Another difference is in comprehension of what is read. You can tell whether it takes you a minute or ten to read a page. But can you always tell whether you have successfully understood the author's meaning? You may think you have and be mistaken. Improving reading skills is not necessarily increasing the speed. Sometimes, the solution is to slow down the fast and careless reader.

The ability to read effectively is related to several conditions. It is a normal tendency to develop those skills in which we already have a degree of proficiency and to ignore those that are weak. For example, if you are athletic and especially good at swimming, you are likely to swim and practice a lot. But if you are not athletic, you probably won't swim much. A good reader tends to read more than a poor one, therefore increasing his proficiency, while a poor reader avoids reading and his skill therefore does not develop.

Reading is easier than listening. One reason is that when we are reading we can proceed at our own pace and if our mind wanders, we can go back and reread. We do not have to adjust to someone else's pace but can proceed at whatever rate enhances our comprehension of the material. Reading provides the opportunity to pause and contemplate the author's message or to look up words that are unfamiliar. Reading also affords us the opportunity to receive the message at a time that is best suited for us.

The Listening Skill

No other communication skill has received more attention from communication specialists recently than that of listening. However, many managers, when they have their choice, will select a course in speaking effectively instead of one in listening. It is also evident that instruction in reading is more popular than that in listening. Opportunities for listening instruction have become more available only in the last few years. Part of this is certainly due to the fact that most of us do not regard ourselves as poor listeners who are in need of instruction.

A poor speaker finds out about his disability quickly. When his audience falls asleep or when the person he is trying to persuade fails to respond, it is easy for him to conclude that his speaking skills are deficient.

By contrast, poor listening ability is harder to detect in oneself. The receiver of a verbal message exerts control over our speaking, but only the listener can check up on his listening skill. Since listening seems as natural as breathing, unless a person is deaf, it is difficult for us to believe that listening abilities are learned.

One of the common misconceptions about listening is the notion that since we can hear, we also can listen. But hearing is an ability that we are born with while listening is something we must learn. Hearing involves the ears while listening involves the mind. Because so many have accepted misconceptions about listening, very little, if any, training has been offered to us. If your listening training was like ours it was very brief and went something like this: "Be quiet and listen."

Recall that meeting of your civic club when you listened to a long speech by one of the city's fathers talking about some long-range goals for the city. You listened at first, but the long account of past developments did not really interest you. You tuned out and began to think about an incident which you were to deal with in the afternoon. You checked back in on the speech about a minute later, and after listening for approximately ten seconds you found the speaker was still on the same old subject, so you went back to contemplating your problem.

You are now in a familiar pattern—a kind of hop-and-skip listening technique. The only trouble is that when you checked back in toward the end of the speech you heard the speaker say, "This tax increase, although heavy, will be willingly born by such civic-minded men and women as you." That was the end of the speech! What did he say, you almost say out loud. "A new tax? Or was it a tax increase? How did I miss that?" Later, as you are driving back to work you have only a vague idea about this important subject, and you secretly hope that no one questions you about what was said.

Of course it was the speaker's fault, you figure. If he wasn't so pompous and would just talk person-to-person rather than making an oration, he might expect us to understand what he has to say. He must think he's a politician or at least he's planning on becoming one! All those big words. You shake your head and try to clear your mind of that incident and focus your attention on what you must say when you bring the people together who are causing the problem at work.

This example illustrates how one can hear a speaker and yet not listen to what he has to say. In this illustration your listening behavior was all too typical of the way most of us listen. How many times have you sat in a group meeting tuning in and out of the discussion, perhaps aware of the general drift but not following the details? If you only superficially hear what a speaker says you may have just a collection of sounds. Effective listening is hard work and requires energetic concentration.

What Is Listening?

Listening consists of a number of dimensions. The first one is that listening is a complex and unique function of perception. Listening is a selective process in that we choose from the many stimuli surrounding us those most fitted to our needs and purposes. Listening develops in three levels. We listen to some stimuli because of their suddenness, intensity, or contrast. There are also stimuli that we have trained ourselves to listen to or virtually force ourselves to listen to. There are those sounds and ideas that we listen to automatically, while on the other hand, there are sounds that we have trained ourselves not to hear. The story is told of the lighthouse keeper who, in addition to his flashing light, also had a gun that automatically went off at regular intervals to warn sailors that they were getting close to the rocky shore. One night the gun failed to go off; and the keeper woke up with a start and said, "What was that?"

The second dimension of listening is that it is a constantly shifting process. This was illustrated in the example of the manager "listening" to a speech. The hop-and-skip approach is a listening technique that we unwisely engage in much too frequently. As adult human beings, we cannot seem to focus on one stimulus for more than a few seconds at a time. Our senses constantly scan the incoming stimuli to find those that carry information of importance or interest to us at a given moment, so we are actually paying attention only in spurts. Sometimes we say to our listeners, "Give me your attention, please." But attention is something not really given; it is earned. Regardless of how important a message may be to us, it is extremely difficult to listen without letting extraneous thoughts enter our minds.

The third dimension of listening that we need to examine is the effect of motives and feelings. Of course our motives, needs, and emotions are always in operation in all communication situations, but they are especially significant when we are listening. We will find a message more valuable if we can determine beforehand what information we want from it. If we have a real need or desire to listen to another person, our listening ability improves remarkably. "The building's on fire! I know the way out! Follow me!" is a message we would want and need to hear; chances are high that we wouldn't miss a word.

When we find that we are unable to focus on something, it may be that we are responding to some hidden feeling or motive that the present stimulus is not satisfying. Another reason listening accurately is difficult is that we often only want to hear certain kinds of information, and we tend not to listen to anything else. It takes a disciplined mind to be aware of one's own desires and expectations and to take them into account in seeking information that may be contradictory or distasteful.

Using feedback in conjunction with listening is a help. As communicators, we should check frequently to see that our receivers are really listening to what we are trying to say. The utilization of feedback for correction is one good way to improve listening. For example, if you expect an employee to be angry when he speaks with you, you are quite likely to hear what he says as angry talk, whether it is or not. Before responding, it would be productive to feed back to the employee the meaning you derived from his words and make certain the anger is really in him and not just in your own perception.

Blocks to Effective Listening

1. **"Just give me the facts."** Attempting to extract only the facts from a spoken message can be confusing and can easily lead to ineffective listening. It is far better to listen for the main points the speaker makes. Those are the points which, in your opinion, represent the

primary themes of the message or the central idea the speaker is trying to impart.

It is impossible for most of us to remember all the facts in any message. By concentrating on the major points, one learns to identify important elements in the speaker's message. The listener who understands the central ideas is also far more likely to remember the facts than the listener who spends his or her listening time cataloging all the possible facts.

2. Being emotionally hypersensitive. Have you ever had the experience of having a single emotionally laden word cause you to tune out the speaker completely? Each of us has our own set of emotionally triggered words and subjects to which we may react or overreact.

We must be aware of those particular words which affect us emotionally and attempt to compensate for them. Try to reduce the effect of these words by developing a defense mechanism against them. Try to repress certain meanings you put on these personal emotionally laden words and substitute new meanings. If you can eliminate a conditioned reaction to a word, you can better determine what meaning the word holds for the speaker.

If, for example, you "see red" whenever the term "liberal" is used, try to hold off your reaction until you thoroughly understand in what sense the speaker is using the word. This technique will enable you to *listen* to the message rather than merely to *hear* the words.

3. Rejection without all the evidence. Many of us, believing that we know in advance that a certain subject will be boring or difficult, close our minds to what is being said. We are then guilty of looking at a very small portion of a total message and rejecting it in its entirety because we disliked the part we heard. If we evaluate a message prematurely and decide we do not need it or want it, we are likely to stop listening and think instead about a golf game or our vacation plans.

4. Standing at attention. Many can remember the experience of standing at attention in the military service. Those who have had such an experience can also recall that being at attention does not necessarily mean that one is paying attention.

Listening attention is easy to fake. By looking or acting as if we are interested, we may fool the speaker into thinking we are listening. But far worse, we may fool ourselves.

What should one do with listening time? Here are some suggestions that might help: (1) Identify the developmental techniques used by the speaker. What examples are used and how are they organized? (2) Review. Use your listening time to review in your mind the points the speaker already has made. This may help your memory as well as your listening. (3) Anticipate what the speaker will say. Be careful with this one, however. This sort of second-guessing can be a bad listening habit if you do not compare what the speaker actually says with what you anticipated he was going to say.

5. Disliking the package or refusing the contents. On occasion we may find we have to listen to people we do not like or whose manner of speaking is distracting. Our listening rapidly deteriorates as we begin to criticize the package the message comes in. In fact, we may miss the contents completely because we dislike the way the package is wrapped.

For example, when a speaker starts to talk, someone might say (or at least think), "Just look at the way that guy stands. Didn't anyone ever tell him not to be walking around so much? And what's more, look how he folds his arms. Listen to the dry way he talks. It's impossible to get anything from a person who sounds like that." This listener can stop listening and feel justified in doing so.

The good listener is more likely to think, "Well, I've heard better speakers for sure, but he has information I can use. I'd better concentrate on what he is saying and forget the manner of speaking." The point is that the message is many times more important than the container in which it comes. When we recognize this simple truth, we are on the way to becoming better listeners. We have thereby accepted at least half of the obligation for the communication process.

Increasing Listening Effectiveness

In addition to eliminating the blocks to effective listening just discussed, there are other techniques we need to master. Basically, effective listening requires that we get inside the speaker's head and that we grasp what he is trying to communicate from *his* point of view. We need to develop the skill of going beyond what we expect a situation to produce and keep testing our expected or anticipated impression against what we actually find in a given statement by another person.

Preparing ourselves to listen is also important. Casual listening is not an effective way to receive vital information. Sometimes we need to convince ourselves ahead of time that there are items of importance to us to be heard in a given situation or from a specific person. We need to develop the attitude that in almost all messages there are likely to be ideas that we can use.

Another technique is to examine the role and purpose of the speaker. Although it is not always possible to determine the speaker's specific purpose, even the effort will make us listen more efficiently.

The quality of the relationship between the speaker and the listener is another important force in the listening process. If we see the speaker as an individual who has much influence on our getting what we want, we will probably not need to exert much effort to listen and respond. Most people find it easier to listen to individuals who have high status and the reputation for credibility. Accurately listening to those with whom we disagree is much harder. For example, try to listen fairly and objectively to campaign speeches made by candidates from a party or position opposed to your own.

Remember that while effective listening is an activity equal in importance to speaking, it is much more difficult to perform. Good listening habits result largely from our mental habits and conditioning. But we can change our habits, and we can profit (literally) by improving our listening abilities.

Although it may appear that we have disproportionately emphasized listening as compared to the other receiving skill, reading, we feel that listening has been for too long the least understood of the skills and the one most likely in need of improvement.

7

Interviewing and Management

So far in this book we have discussed a wide variety of communication elements. By way of review, these include the nature of communication, the self-concept and perception of others and how these influence our interactions with others, the way messages are formulated and meanings are transmitted, the significance of nonverbal behavior, and ways to sharpen various skills.

In the next four chapters we will discuss how these elements function in various kinds of communication structures. We will begin with an exploration of two or more people interacting in the interview; then we will discuss some aspects of small group communication. Next, we will look at the roles of decision-making and problem-solving, and finally we will move to the more complex problems of communication within the organization.

Defining the Interview

A simple definition of an interview is a planned conversation. It is an interaction in which two, and sometimes more, people are engaging in a conversation or dialogue with a purpose. Each participant, that is, is seeking to get or to give information pertaining to a common goal.

Interviewing takes many forms and has many purposes. For instance, you may interview to recruit, to select employees for different jobs, or to reassign employees to new positions. You also may conduct appraisal interviews and exit interviews. Although these types have different specific aims, they all share the same general purpose of seeking information. Information, in this sense, means not only facts, data, and figures, but also feelings, judgments, opinions, and observations.

There are three basic ways of gathering information: (1) by consulting documents, records, books, and other resource materials; (2) through observation of events, objects, or behavior; (3) by interacting with another in face-to-face communication. Often it is through this face-to-face communication that we verify the data collected by the other available means. Frequently the interview is used to interpret the data collected. For example, when evaluating a prospective employee, you may collect data from a variety of sources, but it is very unlikely that you would hire such a person without an interview.

An interview takes place through direct interaction between the seeker of information (the interviewer) and the giver of information (the interviewee). It is a situation where people (usually two, but there may be more) meet to extract and exchange information for a specific purpose. Its success depends on the establishment of effective interaction to accomplish the purpose.

The communication in an interview is different from that of other face-to-face interactions in that it focuses on specific information and attempts to eliminate extraneous messages. Consider the following hypothetical interactions.

You are making your rounds one Monday morning and stop to talk with Will, one of your long-time employees.

You: How are you feeling, Will?
Will: Fine. And you?
You: Pretty good for a Monday, I guess.
Will: Say, did you see the game yesterday?

You: 'Fraid not. Had to take the wife and kids to visit her folks.

Will: Oh, that's too bad. You missed the best game of the year. Suppose we'll make the play-offs?

You: Sure doesn't look like it, does it? Well, I've got to be going. Seen Bill?

Will: Yeah. He was on the floor earlier, but I don't know where he is now.

You leave and find Bill, one of your department heads, in the stockroom, making an inventory check. The following conversation ensues.

You: Hi Bill. How'ya doing?

Bill: Fine.

You: Say, did you ever get the vacation schedule worked out for your department?

Bill: Sure did. Didn't you see it?

You: No. I don't have a copy yet.

Bill: That's funny. I was sure I put one on your desk. Well, I'll get you another one.

You: Good. I need to turn in my report today. Say, how's the new man working out?

Bill: Just fine. He's catching on real good. And he's sure not lazy. He fits in well.

You: Fine. Glad to hear it. Sounds like things are going okay.

Bill: No problems.

You: Good. Take care.

The main difference in these two interactions is that the first had no specific purpose except to be friendly. However, in the second situation the manager was seeking information to meet a specific need. The first is regarded as polite conversation while the second has characteristics of an interview. The manager needed information about two matters: the status of the vacation schedule and an evaluation of a new employee. You, too, use the interview to accomplish a specific purpose while focusing on relevant information and eliminating extraneous data.

This illustration points up another dimension of interviews. Interactions do not have to be formal or specialized to be interviews. Just because we do not call an interaction or dialogue an interview does not mean that the function changes. In fact, you may be involved in some significant interviews without recognizing them as such.

Interviews are such a common part of managerial life that you may have been taking them for granted.

All interviews share some basic characteristics. First, an interview makes certain demands on the person conducting it. He must possess special skills that enable him to achieve the required pattern of interaction. Second, interviewing occurs very frequently and assumes many forms. Last, it is a very important tool.

Managers who complain that "no one ever tells me anything" are revealing that they have not learned how to be either an effective interviewer or interviewee with peers or with employees. On the other hand, one of the most frequent complaints received from unhappy employees is, "I don't know where I stand with my boss," or "My boss never asks me what I think." Too frequently the manager is laboring under the delusion that he or she has satisfactorily communicated with employees. Their dissatisfaction and the manager's lack of awareness of it provide double evidence of the manager's deficiencies as an interviewer.

Earlier we referred to the fact that interviews have a common purpose of information-gathering. In addition to the objective factual data, an interview is also concerned with attitudes, values, feelings, hopes, plans, and descriptions of self. If, for example, you ask an applicant to state his age, his place of birth, and his educational background, this clearly falls within the boundaries of information-gathering. However, you are still gathering information when you include questions designed to learn the applicant's attitude toward his previous job, his aspirations, and his attitude toward your kind of business in general. In the same vein, you may use interviews as a method of inducing an employee to change, through either persuasion or command.

It must be apparent that an interview is not an isolated event; it is usually part of a larger process or a stage in some sequence of events. Thus, the employment interview, the evaluation interview, and the interview to bring about change are all part of an employee's relationship to you and the organization. When you engage in any interview, you must determine just what function the interaction will play in the larger scheme.

Understanding the Interview Process

One important aspect of the process of interviewing involves the meaning of words used in their technical sense, because meanings tend to be somewhat unique to the person using them. A meaning of a word can vary greatly; to discover a word's meaning one must understand the person using it. Recall the earlier discussion about meaning residing in the person rather than the word.

The parties to an interview should also become sensitive to vocal factors and how they can be used to reveal important information in the interview. The ability to "read" physical behavior is also an effective tool of the successful interviewer. (See Chapter Four on nonverbal communication.)

You should consider, whenever possible, the conditions in which the interviewee lives, the persons with whom he associates, and the manner in which he behaves with superiors and subordinates. These factors can provide a clue concerning the nature of the person and can help you evaluate the information you receive.

As an interviewer you should have the ability to relate to the interviewee and to share with him the interview experience, for an interview is a sharing. Both people involved have something to give, and each has the expectation of gaining something from the inter-action. This does not require some sort of special personality. Putting up a false front or trying to create a special image for interviews rarely works. Naturalness is easy to accept; falseness is quite easily detected.

The Art of Asking Questions

The ability to ask effective questions is an art—one which is extremely important. The nature of the questions you put to the interviewee determines to a large extent the quality and depth of information you will be able to gather. Effective questions serve two vital functions: first, they stimulate the interviewee to share information, and, second, they provide him with guidelines as to the nature of information desired from him. By using effective questions, you can control the flow of the dialogue and be certain that you receive valid, relevant, specific, clear, and sufficient information to meet your needs.

Below is an interaction which was used in Chapter Five. This time, pay particular attention to the *quality* of the questions.

Manager: Ted, I'd like to ask you a few questions about our new billing system.
Ted: Sure, shoot.

Manager:	Well, my first question concerns the new system as compared to the old one. Do you think the new system is better?
Ted:	Oh, sure, definitely, It's a big improvement.
Manager:	I'm sure glad of that. Have you had any problems with it?
Ted:	Oh, a few so far. But we found the errors without much trouble.
Manager:	Then the people are happy with it, aren't they?
Ted:	I think so. Don and Paul have been complaining about a few things, but the program is sound.
Manager:	Great. I'm glad everything is going so well. Appreciate your help, Ted. Keep me posted.
Ted:	Sure will. See yah.

We will point out again that this is poor communication. The manager failed to receive the information he needed because of his poor questions and because he did not probe the inadequate responses.

The language of effective questions must be shared by both participants in the interview. The interviewer can make certain that his language is understood through the use of feedback, both verbal and nonverbal. The language of good questions is also economical; excess verbiage is cut out. Look at the following question from a manager to one of his department heads: "Say, Pete, remember that conversation we had the other day, you know, out by the back door, when we were talking about the ah—vacation schedule, ah—, and you said ah, well, that doesn't matter now. I gather that you're able to keep up, or will be, you know, now that you have the new people, ah—, don't you think so?" Somewhere in all that verbiage there must be a question which is supposed to help the manager get the information he needs. But the department head is probably uncertain just what the question is.

Over-elaborating also can be a problem. Although the interviewee undoubtedly can understand an over-explained question, he may resent what appears to be an underestimation of his intelligence. How would you react to this question: "How do you feel about your income tax—that is, the amount you have to pay the federal and state governments on the income you make each year?" You'd probably react negatively because of the implication that you have to have the term "income tax" explained to you. The language of a question must be on a level with that of the interviewee.

Also, the language of the question should be suited to the approach of the interviewer. When the approach is very direct, be very explicit. When the approach is more explorative, such as in appraisal or counseling interviews, the language may be less explicit.

An effective question is relevant to the purpose of the interview. The following conversation occurred in an appraisal interview:

Manager:	Bob, your work has fallen off lately, and if I can be of any help just . . . .
Bob:	Aren't I producing as well as the other guys?
Manager:	Well, yes, of course. But in the past you've always been our top producer.
Bob:	Well, now, if I'm doing my job—I don't get your point.
Manager:	Look, Bob, do you have some problem at home?
Bob:	What the hell has that got to do with anything?

The manager was no doubt trying to be helpful and show that he was personally concerned, but Bob resents the introduction of an irrelevant question—a personal one at that. The manager has raised a communication barrier which will probably end the interaction.

A skilled interviewer avoids questions which lead the interviewee to a particular answer. Contrast the following questions: "How do you feel about the union trying to organize employees?" and "You wouldn't say that you are for the unionization, would you?" Not only is the second version a highly leading question, but if it is asked of a subordinate by a superior, the expected answer can almost be guaranteed. In this case, the question elicits, even encourages, a dishonest answer. Another example of a leading question that is even more subtle might be, "Would you say that you are in favor of the union organizing employees?" The interviewee is being led to answer "yes" if he merely agrees with the wording of the question. It is more difficult to answer "no" because the interviewee would seem to contradict the questioner, or at least to be counter to the ideas of the interviewer.

When interviewers are questioning their subordinates, they should be especially careful to avoid leading questions. Not only does this kind of question (where the hoped-for answer is obvious) tempt people to be dishonest in order not to confront the boss, but less secure employees might, automatically, make whatever response is easiest. Such subordinates seem to be saying, "Tell me what you want me to think." The classic "yes-man" is really of no help to an organization, although the "yes, boss" answer is an employee's only defense against the authoritarian supervisor who, in effect, communicates, "When I want your opinion I'll give it to you!"

Let's say a manager is interviewing a job applicant and learns that the applicant has worked for another store in another state. Since the applicant's former company also has a business in the manager's city, he asks, "I'm not sure I understand. You wanted to return to this city, so was that your reason for leaving your job in Florida? Couldn't you have transferred from the branch in Florida to the branch here?" There are at least two problems with this kind of questioning. First, two questions are asked simultaneously, which will probably result in one going unanswered. Second, both questions are leading. Each begins with an assertion and ends with an invitation to the applicant to agree. This puts pressure on the interviewee to answer "yes." Watch for and eliminate any question which invites a canned answer. Because they are leading questions, they almost ensure unreliable information.

This illustration also underscores the weakness of asking more than one question at a time. Limit questions to a single idea. Notice the presence of two ideas in this otherwise simple question: "And your parents, are they alive and well?" A response of either "yes" or "no" will be completely ambiguous.

The Directive and Nondirective Approaches

As he approaches questioning, the interviewer can assume one of two roles. He may be directive and play a highly dominant role, controlling the flow of information, the speed, and other factors by the manner of questions posed; or he may be nondirective and play a relatively passive role. In this latter approach the interviewee determines, to a considerable extent, what topics are to be discussed, while in the directive approach the respondent is required to answer specific questions. Sometimes these two approaches are referred to as *interviewee-centered* and *interviewer-centered* interviews.

Most skilled interviewers rely on the directive approach when specific information is needed, as in an employment interview or an interview concerning the facts of a given case. The nondirective approach is likely to be beneficial when general feelings and opinions of the interviewee are significant or when there are areas of exploration that can be developed better by the interviewee than by the interviewer. Of course, many interviews require that both approaches be used at different points in the interaction. Above all, the interview is dynamic. It should go without saying that both participants should be flexible and responsive to directive or nondirective methods as the situation and its requirements dictate.

In conjunction with these two approaches, there are two types of questions which seem appropriate: open or closed. For example, an employee says, "This overtime is a pain in the neck. I don't mind a little of it, but it should be spread out more. Some of the others don't get picked half as often as I do." If the interviewer responds with, "You feel that you have been treated unfairly in the assignment of overtime?" he has asked an open question. Such a question mirrors the feelings inherent in the employee's statement. On the other hand, suppose that the interviewer asks, "How often did you work overtime last month?" He has asked a closed question which requests specific data; nothing else would be appropriate. Of course, the closed question may be just the right one to use, depending on the purpose of the interview and who initiated it.

An interviewer should not regard one type of question as better than the other; both have their weaknesses and values. When to use the open question and when to use the closed question depends on the specific purpose of the interview, the kinds of data needed, and the nature of the relationship between the participants in the transaction. In brief, an open question permits the answer to go in many different directions while the closed question seeks a specific bit of information, usually a short answer such as "yes" or "no."

Coping With the Inadequate Response

An inadequate response is one that neither meets the expectations of the interviewer nor helps to accomplish the purpose of the interview. Inadequate responses are usually those that are over-verbalized, irrelevant, inaccurate, partial, ambiguous, or contain no real answer at all. Sometimes questioners get inadequate responses because the interviewee does not understand the purpose of the question or the kind of answer that is required. The actual language used also may be unclear or beyond his comprehension.

The interviewee may not remember the data called for or may feel the question goes beyond the limits of what he or she is willing to reveal to the interviewer. For example, suppose a manager asks an applicant about his spare-time activities or about family relationships. The applicant may feel these questions are inappropriate to the general subject of the interview, or that they deal with matters that he is unwilling to discuss with the interviewer. Similarly, female applicants, rightfully, may be reluctant to answer questions about their marital status or dependents since it is now illegal to ask questions that wouldn't be asked of a man and which have nothing to do with job qualifications.

There are two basic kinds of questions available to the manager in an interview. One is the primary question, which is used to introduce a new topic or to direct the discussion into a new train of thought. No matter how well these questions are worded, they very often fail to receive an adequate response. When this happens, the interviewer should turn to secondary questions or probes to develop the information already asked for by a primary question. Remember the example used earlier in this chapter of the manager asking Ted about the new billing procedure? The manager asked only primary questions, and in every case he received an inadequate response; he failed to use a single secondary or probe question. Of course, it could be that the manager didn't really want to know, and if this was the case, he met his objective.

In coping with the inadequate response the interviewer must try to decide what the underlying causes are. On the basis of this judgment, he then formulates his probe questions. If he is completely in doubt about the causes, he may have to come right out and ask the interviewee. In any case, the inadequate response makes severe demands on the interviewer's skill and judgment. Failure to probe effectively is one of the major causes of ineffective interviewing. Let's look at some examples of how skilled interviewers use probe questions.

Interviewer: Do you expect to finish the work in the back room this week?

Interviewee: Well, I sure hope so. I'm really tired of all the mess and confusion.

Interviewer: I can sure understand that. But, how about your expectations? Do you *expect* the job to be finished this week?

At first glance it may seem that the response was adequate, but are aspirations and expectations the same? Suppose the interviewee's reaction to the last question had been, "Oh, well, that's different. I sure hope we can finish this week, and we are sure going to try; but realistically, I don't expect to be through until Tuesday of next week."

Unless the interviewer had used a secondary question, he might have gone away with an inadequate interpretation of the situation.

Notice that although the interviewer recognizes this as an inadequate response, he accepts the answer and with the second question, makes a transition back to his objective. A good interviewer will not show rejection of the first response but will accept it for what it is and then lead the interviewee to respond in another fashion. In this example it is not that the interviewee did not understand the question or was deliberately avoiding an adequate response. It is more likely that he was preoccupied with other concerns which led him to speak of his "hopes" rather than his "expectations."

Many times the response will be inadequate because the interviewee has difficulty verbalizing. The difficulty may occur because the interviewee is asked about an issue on which he has not yet formulated an opinion or because he is defensive about the subject. The following example, in which Mrs. Henderson is the supervisor and Henry Schultz is the employee, illustrates these kinds of problems.

Mrs. Henderson:	On the whole, would you say you are satisfied with your present job or would you like to try the assignment in the new department?
Henry:	Well, like, I don't know what to say. The pay is good in this job, but, ah—and I sure like the people in this department. But sometimes, you know, it gets pretty routine and monotonous, and—I wonder, I feel that I'm not, you know, getting ahead as fast in this department as I thought I would.
Mrs. Henderson:	There are things on both sides. You feel undecided?
Henry:	Yeah, and that's a fact. It's sure a tough kind of a decision to have to make. I think though—I think that when you consider everything together, I would really like to have a chance at the other job, particularly if there is a chance to become a supervisor someday.

Notice particularly the interviewer's statement, "You feel undecided." This statement suggests she recognizes the ambivalence and gives the employee a chance to think it through. This is a nondirective approach which encourages further discussion. A direct approach in this case would have been ineffective.

The following dialogue illustrates how a detective, using probing techniques, helps a holdup victim remember details.

Detective:	Now, Mr. Rodgers, I understand you were in the establishment when it was held up. Will you tell me what happened?
Mr. Rodgers:	Yeah, sure, I'll try. You see, this man came in, and the first I knew anything about it, he shouted, "This is a stickup!" And he was waving this pistol around and that was the biggest gun I ever saw.
Detective:	Can you describe the man for me; what did he look like?
Mr. Rodgers:	Oh, gosh, I don't know. You see, I'm afraid I don't remember too much about what happened.
Detective:	Well, give me as much information as you can. Anything at all will help. Do you remember anything?
Mr. Rodgers:	Well, let me see. I'd say he was about middle-aged, and kind of skinny. I can't remember too much else because I was pretty scared. I'll never forget though how when I turned around, and he was looking me right straight in the eye. Man, I froze.
Detective:	I can understand. It's hard to remember too well in situations like this. How old would you say he was?
Mr. Rodgers:	Well, I'm not sure. Somewhere between 40 and 60 I'd say.
Detective:	Somewhere between 40 and 60. Which would you say would be closer?
Mr. Rodgers:	I don't know. I remember he had some gray hair, but not much, so I'd say about 45 or 46.

By using a series of appropriate probes, the detective is able to get Mr. Rodgers to think about the age of the robber and come up with a reasonably specific answer.

As the interview continues, the detective is able to help the holdup victim remember a surprising number of details. His technique is to accept the confusion which Mr. Rodgers feels and assure him that he understands his problem of trying to describe an individual who was seen so briefly and under such stressful circumstances.

By using probes skillfully, the interviewer can motivate the interviewee to verbalize his feelings and observations. Effective probes must be nonjudgmental, conveying neither positive nor negative interviewer opinions on the topic under discussion. This will stimulate the interviewee to respond to rather than retard the interaction.

On Being the Interviewer

Although at least two people are required in order to conduct an interview, most of the attention is usually focused on the interviewer since he or she is the one who normally initiates the interaction. In this section we will look more closely at the special role of the interviewer, and in the following section, we will investigate the role of the manager as interviewee.

When the manager is in the role of interviewer, there are several things he needs to do or become aware of. First, if possible, he should know the interviewee. Even with individuals we know very well, a particular situation such as an interview can alter what we think we know. The manager should at least try to anticipate what the interviewee will be like in this specific situation. What will be his thoughts, attitudes, feelings? What will be the interviewee's perception of the interview? Managers should try to project themselves into the situation the interviewee faces. If the manager can predict how the interviewee will feel and how he will perceive the situation, he will do a better job of adjusting the communication level and creating an appropriate climate for effective interaction.

As a manager, you should also try to determine how friendly the interaction should be. How "friendly" is "too friendly" is difficult to measure, but when it reaches the point where it inhibits the purpose of the interview, the "closeness" is too great. We are not suggesting that a certain psychological distance from the interviewee be maintained constantly. Sometimes a high level of interpersonal involvement is essential to reach the necessary levels of acceptance that will permit the interviewee to open up.

A good interviewer often finds it necessary to conform to the customs and norms of the interviewee without making a value judgment. This may put the interviewee at ease and eliminate the barriers to revealing vital information. For example, an interviewee whose values lead him to deplore profanity will not respond well to an interviewer who uses it. Even a simple matter like smoking during the interview may inhibit the effectiveness of the interaction.

Have a clear purpose and share it with the interviewee. In addition, let him know the area or nature of information which is needed and the reason for it. If possible, communicate this to the other person early so he can prepare, consult documents, or bring the necessary material with him.

A good interviewer controls and focuses the interview toward his specific objectives. Often misunderstood, the word "control" leads many to believe the interviewer should completely dominate the interaction. On the contrary; control is not manipulation of the interviewee, nor is it slavishly following a predetermined outline. Once the purpose is established and accepted, the interviewee may profitably move forward on his own. An interviewer loses vital information when he tries too hard to control or restrict the course of the discussion. It should not be overlooked, however, that some interviewees need more control than others. For example, a dependent person feels more at ease and more secure in an authoritarian atmosphere while the more independent person requires less control and feels more secure in a democratic situation.

It also may be necessary to correct any misconceptions the interviewee may have about the function and purpose of the interview. You probably can remember having been asked to meet with a superior with no idea given about the nature of the meeting. It is likely that as you approached such a situation, you reviewed all your past sins and shortcomings and wondered just which one had been detected. Maybe you even began to prepare your defense as well as you could. When you finally appeared at the appointed time you may have found that the purpose of the meeting was vastly different from what you feared; perhaps you were to be congratulated instead of chastised. The interviewee should be made aware of his function in the interview as early as possible, preferably when the original arrangements are made.

The creation of an atmosphere in which the interviewee feels that he is understood and in which he can communicate comfortably is also the function of the interviewer. But how does one "create" such an atmosphere? First, you do some things to set the stage so that the person will feel secure and relaxed. Try to provide the best possible setting. Sometimes this may be difficult, but the location doesn't always have to be your office. Wherever the interview is held, it should afford as much privacy as the nature and purpose of the interview require. Try to avoid such physical barriers as desks and tables located between interviewer and interviewee because such barriers heighten the interviewer's dominant status and may increase feelings of tension. The scene of one person behind a desk and another in front of it is reminiscent of the encounter in the principal's office and, unless your experience was significantly different from ours, you will recall this as a not-too-pleasant confrontation.

The setting should be free of tension-producing items. Unfamiliar objects produce tension; forms and recording equipment which you may be using during the interview should be explained. The same is true of other people in the room. If you have a colleague present, introduce him and clarify the reason for his presence. It's never a good idea to give the interviewee the impression that he is being double-teamed or secretly evaluated. No one likes to feel outnumbered.

As far as possible, the interview should be held without interference from outside sources, such as ringing telephones or conversations with other persons about matters not related to the interview. Creation of an atmosphere of acceptance and safety is of great significance because the interviewee needs to feel free from serious threats to his ego. He should feel that his integrity is respected and that you really want to listen to what he has to say. When an interviewee feels these dimensions present, you have created a good atmosphere.

The timing of questions and transitions is also an important interviewer skill. Asking a "good" question at the "wrong" time may destroy its value. An effective manager senses when an employee needs help or coaching and when to hold back. An interviewer skilled in good timing has a sense of when to do something or say something that will bring the most desirable results. Try to determine the mood of the interviewee, his expectation of what is coming, his desire to respond, his readiness to follow your lead, his ability to provide the needed information, his degree of physical fatigue, his perception of freedom to speak frankly, and his desire to be helpful. Of course, timing is a combination of many factors, all of which hinge on the interviewer's own sensitivity to all forces involved.

We have already written at length about the role of listening in interpersonal communication. Too often the skill of asking questions, or talking, is stressed in the training of interviewers without explaining that the listening role may really be the more important skill. Transcripts of many managers' interviews indicate that they tend to fill the majority of the time with what they themselves have to say. Often the interviewee is limited to brief responses to direct questions. This may tell the interviewee a great deal about the manager, but it doesn't give the manager much of a chance to learn about the other person. Recordings or transcripts of interviews by professional interviewers, on the other hand, usually reveal a preponderance of talk by the interviewee. The interviewer provides topics and questions that stimulate the interviewee to respond, and the interviewer devotes most of his time to listening. Of course, if the purpose of the interview is to transmit information, the interviewer takes the necessary time to do so, but he allows time for feedback. He encourages the interviewee to seek clarification.

Listening in these situations occurs on three levels. Visually, you can observe the reactions of the interviewee; aurally, you hear what is being said; and, physically, you adjust your body in a way that demonstrates to the interviewee that he is being listened to. Any listening skill you can develop for yourself that enables you to perceive more accurately and to remember more thoroughly will be of great value.

Although professional interviewers accurately record what is said, this does not mean that they write excessively during the interview. In fact, writing should be held to a minimum. This is true for several reasons: It is distracting to both parties; pauses for writing tend to chop the interview into disconnected parts; the notes are based on the writer's impressions at that particular time and may not be an accurate evaluation of the whole; and notes tend to heighten the tension of the interviewee.

Nevertheless, you must have some record of what is said in most interview situations. The best rule seems to be to make summarized notes at the end. This allows you to consider the interview in its entirety. Mentally, you edit out the unimportant and focus your summary on the most significant elements. In this way you can deal with dominant impressions rather than with instant reactions. True impressions can be more carefully drawn and are more likely to be understood when referred to later.

Granted there are occasions when it is desirable to note a key word or fact during the interview. It is best not to do this when you or the interviewee is talking, however. Pause, let the interviewee know that you consider a bit of information important and let him know what you are doing by saying something like, "That's important. I'd better make sure that I remember it correctly. Excuse me while I make a note of it."

Whatever procedure is used, the record should be accurate and as complete as necessary for your purpose. Use of feedback during the interview can help assure accuracy. By checking perceptions with the interviewee you can correct any errors in your understanding of what was said.

In summary, the role of the effective interviewer is multidimensional. He or she must establish a favorable atmosphere for the interaction, help the interviewee function in his role, maximize the elements leading to effective communication, reduce or eliminate any barriers that might impede the flow of dialogue, and direct or steer the conversation in such a way that the interview may best accomplish the purpose for which it was intended. This is not easy, but proficiency in interviewing can be learned.

On Being the Interviewee

For an interview to reach its objectives effectively, both participants must perform their roles adequately. We have just analyzed the interviewer's part; now we must deal with the other person in the transaction. Frequently it is assumed that if a person functions well in the role of interviewer, he or she can also function effectively as an interviewee. But this is not necessarily the case. Consider the following dialogue.

Sandy Pitman, who works for Charles Howard, has just been passed over for a promotion. She also has been informed that she has been scheduled for a transfer to a new department and a different job. Sandy considers both events unfair. She makes an appointment to see Mr Howard.

Sandy: May I come in?

Mr. H.: Sure, come on in, Sandy. Sit down. Now, what did you have on your mind?

Sandy: Well, I got to thinking about what you said in the meeting the other day, about talking to you if something was bugging us, or there was something we didn't understand. Well, I thought I'd let you know that I'm very upset, and, ah—I don't understand it.

Mr. H.: Why don't you tell me about it? Maybe I can help.

Sandy: It's two things. Getting turned down for that promotion, and now I'm told that I have to work under Mr. Hilton, in his department. What's this outfit got against me, anyway? I thought I was doing pretty good, and well, now this. And I don't mind telling you I'm upset.

Mr. H.:	I'm sorry you feel that way. But it's history now and there is nothing I can do about it. There'll be other chances for promotion.
Sandy:	Well, maybe, but damn it, this thing is bugging me and I . . .
Mr H.:	Now wait a minute, Sandy. This isn't getting us anywhere. The appointment has been made and getting worked up now isn't going to help. Is there anything else on your mind?
Sandy:	Moving me to another department. That's not history, yet. It's been scheduled, but it hasn't gone into effect yet.
Mr. H.:	I believe you're judging that too soon. I think that job is right down your alley
Sandy:	Well, I don't like it. Nobody asked me! And I don't like all the politics around this outfit that will stick a hardworking and faithful person like me in a place like . . .
Mr. H.:	What do you mean, "politics?"
Sandy:	You know what I mean. That promotion should have been given to me and not that young Bill White. If it wasn't for all his . . .
Mr. H.:	Now hold on there just a darn minute, Sandra. If you can't talk about this matter without getting into personalities . . .
Sandy:	For heaven's sake, that's the point. Personalities are what it's all about! That's what I came in here to talk to you about. I've been trying to tell you that . . .
Mr. H.:	Wait a minute. I don't like the tone of your voice. You've got no right to come in here and run down a good man and bad-mouth this whole organization with your childish charge of politics. If you can't talk these things over in a calm and civilized . . .

And so on and so forth. Most of us dislike situations like this one—no matter which role we are in. *It's quite possible that Mr. Howard did not realize he was the interviewee in this encounter.* Sandy had initiated the interview; she had specific objectives she wanted met, and she needed certain information. Of course, she did a poor job. But because Mr. Howard was the manager, he must take most of the responsibility for the disaster. He seemed more concerned with maintaining his status and power and in defending the organization than he was in meeting the objectives of the interview.

What can you, as the interviewee, do to make the process effective? First, find out what the interview is about. When Sandy asked for an appointment with Mr. Howard, it would have been desirable for him to know about the nature of her visit so he could have been better prepared.

You should also be willing to communicate what you know while at the same time making known any areas you do not wish to discuss, as long as you give reasons for your position. As with those occasions when you are the interviewer, there are times when you will need to prepare. Try to have the necessary information and supporting documents handy. It is wise to be sure of your information and provide sources and origins. On the other hand, if you have doubts about some idea or about the accuracy or consistency of your data, point this out.

Make time available for the interview by trying to learn how long it is likely to run; then schedule accordingly. Nothing turns off an employee more than feeling that you do not have enough time to talk with him about his problems. If there really is not time available, explain this and schedule the interview for a better time. During the interview, always be conscious of time limitations and watch for clues from the interviewer that will signal that the time allotted has expired. Rarely do you enhance your position by attempting to extend an interview beyond the time the interviewer expects it to go.

Finally, always attempt to correct and prevent misunderstandings. Do this by asking for feedback so you can be sure that what the interviewer understands is actually what you said and meant him to understand. It is just as much your job as the interviewer's to see that the right information is transmitted and received. Do everything possible to see that what you say is accurately received and, if possible, recorded.

As we have seen, interviewing is an interaction process that involves at least two people. The interview has been described as conversation with a purpose, but it has both formal and informal dimensions. Informally, it is used to gather information in brief encounters which, heretofore, you may not even have regarded as interviews. Formally, you know interviews as employment, appraisal, reprimand, counseling, or orientation interviews. Skillful managers will be aware that at times they are almost as likely to take on the role of the interviewee as that of the interviewer. They should not underestimate the talents and skills required on either side of the interview process.

8
Making the Most of Meetings

In this chapter we are concerned with the role meetings play in management and operations. In our conversations with managers, we found differences in opinion about the importance of meetings and group discussions in the overall operation. Some feel that there are too many meetings and that too much time is wasted this way. Others describe their group discussions as prime opportunities for shared decision-making and better communication.

Meetings do seem to be essential to effective organizations. It is doubtful that an organization could survive very well without them, in our view. However, meetings can, and should, be improved. Much of the criticism leveled against group discussions stems from a lack of understanding of crucial group forces and the complexities of leadership. The naive manager thinks all he or she has to do to have a meeting is to gather people together.

Since the meeting is so important, it is no wonder that extensive research on this subject has been conducted in the last 20 years or that many companies conduct training programs in group dynamics and leadership. In this chapter, we will discuss some of this theory and make specific suggestions as to how it may be applied to managerial operations.

When we realize the interacting nature and multiple communication objectives in modern organizations, it is easy to understand the significance of all the various meetings. They give participants an opportunity to interact and develop into an effective team. Employees can share their experiences, problems, and successes. Meetings also serve as a channel for upward communication, briefing upper levels of management on information about and from employees throughout the system. The meeting, properly conducted, is the one vehicle that can best accomplish most communication and managerial purposes at one time. It can serve to keep people informed, to solve problems and make decisions, to discover attitudes, and to provide a participative medium and climate. As a manager, you may very well find yourself applying more of the principles of communication in meetings than in any other managerial activity.

At this point in the book we are shifting from one-to-one communication to one-to-a-few or one-to-many communication. But we should keep in mind that even the one-to-many communicator (such as a speaker to a large audience or over television) does not communicate with a "mass," but rather to one person at a time. Messages are never received by groups, only individuals. So, although we are shifting context, we are still talking about *interpersonal* communication.

Let's take a close look at some of the reasons modern business and industry rely so heavily on group meetings. In recent years there has been a shift to more democratic leadership in which the manager has come to see him- or herself less as a boss and more as a leader of a team. The focus has shifted from the concept of "managing a business" to that of "managing people." And the manager must not only manage individuals but also direct a "work group." This view does not suggest that the manager should ignore individuals, but it does mean that in addition to employing the skill of working with individuals, the manager must also be concerned with people as a group, with forming subordinates into a well-functioning team.

In the modern organization the emphasis is on giving more participative opportunities to employees, encouraging group decision-making with subordinates, and establishing a more comfortable work climate. No wonder so much research and training in this one area has been conducted in recent years. The necessary changes in attitudes and managerial skills have been astounding.

Why Meetings?

Clearly, the organizational meeting is well-suited to serve a number of important purposes. First, a meeting is basically a pooling together of information, knowledge, facts, opinions, and judgments of participants in order to accomplish a specific purpose. Often when a meeting is called it is for the purpose of solving a problem. It has long been believed, and current research supports this, that two or more heads are better than one in solving problems. Decision-making and policy-making are also purposes of many managerial meetings, for rarely do we find today's managers or supervisors making decisions without involving others at some point in the process.

Other important functions of the meeting are to inform and instruct members. As a manager you may have certain information which you have received from your superiors in the organization, and this data must be passed along. A meeting is the appropriate place for this transfer of information.

A new plan or policy established by the personnel division also calls for a meeting in which all employees can be informed at the same time, in the same way. The staff meeting is ideal for this since it is an opportunity for questions, discussions, feedback, and clarification.

The training meeting is a standard method in many organizations for developing the abilities of employees. Such areas as teaching new procedures, orienting new employees, or changing ordering and reporting methods are all good subjects for group training meetings.

Meetings can be identified by type as well as purpose. One type is the staff meeting which includes all persons who are subordinate to one particular manager or leader. This group might include the members of a department who report to a unit head or a group of unit heads who report to a company officer at a higher level. In most organizations these are "regular" meetings which can be convened for a variety of purposes.

Committees: Keeping Minutes, Wasting Hours?

The fact that meetings are necessary and are used extensively does not mean that they are always effective. One hears complaints about the frustration caused by meetings. When these complaints are analyzed, it often is discovered that many meetings are badly organized and poorly conducted and, therefore, totally useless. You do not have to attend many meetings like this to conclude either that your company is holding too many meetings or the leaders do not know how to use a meeting effectively.

It is not unusual for the meeting which wastes time to have had as its original purpose the saving of time. What goes wrong at such meetings? It could be that the manager rushes into the meeting with everything planned (probably too much for one meeting), and opens the meeting with an apology for having called it. He promises the group the meeting will end promptly at a given time because he knows several people have meetings and appointments at that time; in fact, he too has to attend another meeting following this one. Everything about him has communicated haste. Maybe he is the type who glances at his watch when someone begins to speak about something. Or when a discussion develops he cuts it off with a reminder that time is passing and there are so many items to be covered.

The individual who interrupts this steamrolling affair to ask a question or contribute information is a brave and possibly a foolhardy person. The members quickly learn that speed is more important than getting the work done effectively or making the best possible decision. The leader goes through the motions of discussing the items on the agenda and asking questions which no one feels free to explore; no real communication takes place. Participation is stifled by the compulsive drive to cover the agenda and to do so in the specified time. Such a meeting is useless, and should never have been called.

Some organizations continue to hold meetings out of habit rather than need. At one time there probably was a purpose to these meetings, but now the group seems incapable of recognizing that the need no longer exists.

Another kind of useless meeting is the one in which the leader uses the meeting to conceal his decision. Having already made up his mind, he pretends that the meeting has been called to discuss the problem and arrive at a solution. As a rule, it does not take long for employees to catch on to the fact that their primary function in such a meeting is to act as a rubber-stamp and that the meeting is a sham. They will realize that there is no point in discussing the issues or seeking to solve an already solved problem.

Group Meetings—What Are They?

The group meeting is a dynamic process which is fluid, inexact, changing, and impossible to reduce to a set of patterns and descriptions. These qualities should not be regarded as negative, but rather as a meeting's chief assets. Since these characteristics do not permit the use of gimmicks or a set of procedural rules, we must depend on our judgment in application of communication principles in a wide variety of situations. Any group of people, coming together to pool their knowledge and opinions, needs and hopes, trusts and fears, creates an exceedingly dynamic phenomenon. A group is never static; it changes from minute to minute as the interaction unfolds.

Just the potential for interaction is overwhelming. Consider the possible relationships in a group with ten members. Take just one member and determine the possible interrelationships he or she has with the other nine, and then go to the next person. Each relationship is unique, and each has its own characteristic form of interaction. Whenever people come together, for whatever reason, there is a potential for this dynamic interaction. Decisions can be made; needs can be met; policies can be established; friendships or hostilities can develop. The more you as the manager know about how people operate in groups, the greater your potential for accomplishing effective group behavior.

A meeting consists of a group of people and is an entity with a style and personality all its own. It is made up of individual human beings, each of whom brings to the meeting his or her own personality, values, feelings, and needs. When these individuals combine in a meeting, they become something more than the sum total of the individual members. Each person influences the others and, in turn, is influenced by them. The group acquires characteristics which result from the interaction of the members. This "group personality" will influence the way in which the members will participate and relate to each other. One cannot "know" a group by studying the individual members outside of the group.

Every group develops its own *norms*. These are expectations of how participants should behave, codes of conduct, or standards for participation. Norms reflect and determine how we speak, to whom we speak, how we dress, where and how we sit, what we talk about, what sentiments we share, how we express them, and so forth. Norms are implicit rules which are rarely stated out loud. Conformity to norms is essential if members are to work together. If your group meets regularly at a given time or place, this is an established norm. If people arriving late feel called upon to apologize or explain, you have established another norm. Basically, norms are the unwritten bylaws.

One of the first tasks of a new group member is to learn the norms, for groups have ways of punishing members who violate their norms or try to break established patterns. The more a person prizes membership in a group, the more he or she will conform. New employees who are told, "No, not *that* way; we do things *this* way around here," learn they have collided with a company or group norm.

On Being the Leader

There are those who view a group of people in the same way they view a machine. Just as the operator of a machine can manipulate the function by operating various switches or levers to bring about a predetermined level of performance, so can the leader manipulate people and get the group to do exactly what he wants. These cynics take comfort in the fact that a machine does not react to the personality of the operator, but only to his skills.

We all know that people are not machines, and there are no levers to push to produce effective interaction or problem-solving. What's more, the wise leader is aware that group success is at least in part a function of how the members see him as a human being and is not related just to his directions and orders.

Most of us know that the status or authority of a leader will not completely assure a desired response. Yet this notion persists. Giving orders or directives and supplying facts or data do not comprise leadership, but they often pass for such.

There is no person more important to the success of a group meeting than the one at the top. If the leader's job is to gain meaningful response from people, he must effectively relate to them. "I am their leader, but I can't get them to follow me!" comes from a person who sees the group in the same light as he sees a machine. The point is that the leader's attitude about people may be far more important than his repertory of skills and techniques. The leader who best serves his group and his organization is one who has both a positive attitude about people and the ability to get things done with the help of others. Good leaders are known by the people they develop rather than the ones they dominate.

As a leader of a meeting you have three basic responsibilities: to guide, stimulate, and control. You guide by organizing an agenda and following it, by proceeding clearly from one question or subject to another, by making clear transitions and summaries, and by keeping the discussion from straying too far from the subject. (Some tangents can be productive, so we shouldn't hold too tight a rein.) You stimulate by creating an atmosphere in which others will feel they want to participate. You make certain that all have the opportunity to participate by inviting silent members to join in, by raising appropriate and clear questions, and by presenting data which you may have. You control the meeting by seeing to it that the purpose of the meeting is accomplished. To do this you may have to move the discussion along from a subject the group would rather stay with. You may have to move toward the evaluative stage of the proposed solutions before the members have exhausted the identification of all possible solutions. And as you do all these things with tact and finesse, you must be careful not to dominate the discussion on the one hand or be too permissive and let the interaction wander aimlessly on the other.

Planning for the Meeting

One of the first considerations to confront is the question of the need for the meeting. Do not have a meeting unless it is necessary. Nothing destroys the effectiveness of meetings like the overuse of them. But when meetings are necessary, how should they be prepared for? Most of the steps in preparing for a meeting are relatively simple, but the failure to complete them may cause problems. Do not make the mistake of waiting until the last minute to plan. We have known leaders who were late to meetings because of last minute preparations; all they accomplished was communicating a negative attitude about the gathering's importance.

Here are the major steps in planning:

1. Determine the purpose of the meeting and communicate it to the participants. Is it to solve a problem, make a decision, give instructions or information, or a combination of all of these?

If the meeting is more ritualistic than functional, the participants should know so that they will have realistic expectations. If the meeting is to be creative, then it must be conducted in such a way that a strong climate of free-wheeling permissiveness is developed. Think how it affects you to believe that a meeting is called as a decision-making session, and after you have done a lot of preparation you discover that the decision will be made later, or even worse, that it has already been made. Do everything in your power to make certain that all members understand the purpose of the meeting. If it becomes necessary to change the purpose, let this be known.

2. Prepare the agenda. This is basically a listing of the subjects to be covered. Many meetings have only one item on the agenda, and if the group is small and its members work together regularly, this step will need little attention. But more often a meeting will be called to consider several matters.

An effective agenda reflects not only what will be discussed but also in what sequence and about how much time is expected to be devoted to each item. Prior consideration should also be given to the extent you wish the group to participate on each subject. On some items you may be seeking advice only, while on others you may want the decision to be made by the group. Leaders use a variety of methods to determine the matters which should be considered in any given meeting. Whatever your method, it should, in most cases, be known by the members well in advance of the meeting. Ideally, group members should feel free to suggest agenda items of their own either before or during the meeting.

3. Arrange for a meeting place. What is the best place for a meeting? Many factors enter into this decision. If the meeting is ritualistic, use the most impressive conference room you have or arrange for an appropriate room somewhere in the community. On the other hand, it is better to avoid the office of a high-status member if you are holding a decision-making meeting. This kind of room may inhibit the free flow of communication required.

In selecting the meeting place, choose one that is compatible with your purpose. For example, a very effective meeting may occur as a kind of huddle in the back room when the purpose is to the point and can be resolved in a few minutes. In general, choose a small, simple meeting room with few distractions where the members can sit close enough together to see and hear each other easily.

Leading the Meeting

Having looked at some of the preparation needed before the meeting begins, now let's look at what should be done during the course of the meeting. Earlier we said that leadership involved the functions of guiding, stimulating, and controlling the interaction. To accomplish these, you should be open-minded and group-centered, not dogmatic and self-centered. Your manner should be pleasant, enthusiastic, and tactful; you should be a good listener and an effective communicator. In addition, it is important to know something about the dynamics of groups, how cohesiveness is formed, and how to move the group to a decision.

Guiding the meeting involves seeing that its purpose is accomplished by efficiently covering the agenda. When the agenda requires you to explain, instruct, or inform, you should plan for this even to the point of making a short speech. There is nothing wrong with this as long as information-giving is the goal and purpose. You should be sure, however, that the group understands this and that the participants have the opportunity to ask questions and to discuss the matter after your presentation. Don't make a speech in the group meeting unless it is the most efficient and effective means of reaching the objectives.

A more difficult guiding problem occurs in the problem-solving group. A part of the difficulty is that you may not have a clear picture of just how the group should proceed. The "Systematic Approach to Problem-Solving" which will be presented in Chapter Nine is applicable to groups as well as individuals. There is a tendency for groups, just as for individuals, to pass over certain steps or to spend too much time on some, or to start seeking solutions before they fully understand the problem. By asking questions and calling for suggestions you can keep the group on target. Be careful, however, that you do not become so concerned with structure that it destroys creativity and spontaneity.

Stimulating the group is the process of keeping the group members interested, motivated, and participating. Your primary tool for this, in addition to your own manner, attitude, and personality, is the use of questions. Because the art of asking questions is itself such a vital function of leadership, a later section of this chapter will be devoted to this subject.

Good leaders control the meeting so that it may accomplish its purpose. At the same time they are aware of the passing of time in order to see that it is used effectively. Part of controlling, however, is to prevent the group from moving too fast. As you do all these things, some may say you are exercising too much control. Make sure you are doing the best you can under the circumstances. The criticism may be due to the way you exercise control rather than the control itself. The group will not be overly critical if they perceive you are trying to be both democratic and efficient and to do what is best for the organization.

In trying to keep the discussion moving, watch for signs that a given item has been discussed enough. Apparent loss of interest or drifting from the subject are clues that the time has come to stop talking about a topic. The summary is the most useful technique at this point to help you round off the consideration of an item and lead naturally to the next topic. Also, ask whether enough time has been devoted to the subject and if the group would like to move to the next item.

Discussion Questions

Questions can be categorized several ways. There are *questions of fact,* those that seek facts and information or that attempt to find a "factual" answer to a broad question. Some questions of this type might be: "When did this problem start?"; "How many people are involved?"; "Who was working when the accident happened?"

Questions of interpretation inquire about the meaning of facts or information. Some examples would be: "How do you explain the fact that . . .?" or "How can we interpret this report from the head office?"

Then there are the *questions of value* which ask the respondent for his judgment or opinion. When the question, "How serious is this problem?" is asked it calls for a judgment because "serious" is a value-judgment word. But in support of his position on the matter the respondent will likely supply facts or information. The leader must be able to tell the difference and distinguish between fact and opinion. Some other questions of this type might be: "How good is this new plan?"; "Why do you think it is best?"; "Will it solve our problem?"; "Should we accept the union's offer?"

In problem-solving discussions, questions of fact are most useful in the early stages when the focus in on problem analysis. Questions of value are used most often in the later stages of evaluating solutions and arriving at the best solution or decision. Questions of interpretation are used throughout.

Questions may also be classified according to whether they are asked as *general* or *rhetorical* questions. One of the uses of the general question is to get the discussion started. It is placed before the participants in the hope that someone will pick it up and begin to explore the subject. This type of question can also be used as a means of getting someone to summarize what has been accomplished up to a given point. Examples of this sort of question are: "I've explained the problem as I see it. Does anyone see it differently?" or "We've discussed many angles of this situation. Would anyone care to summarize what we have discovered so far?"

As we know, rhetorical questions are asked to stimulate thought rather than to elicit a specific answer. They are used to arouse interest, to focus attention, or to suggest that the group think differently or more deeply. Some examples of this type: "Certainly we enjoyed a prosperous year. But I wonder what adjustments might we have to make if the present economic conditions continue?"; "Participative management sounds good in theory, but some things are not clear in my mind. Where would we draw the line on employees participating in policy- or decision-making? Is there such a thing as partial democracy? Can we be sure they won't want to intrude in areas that management considers its prerogative?" A rhetorical question generally begins with a statement or assertion, such as, "Participative management sounds good . . .," which is then followed by a question or questions about it. Although it does not require an answer at the time it is presented, it may well require that the matter be considered eventually as the group deliberates.

Leaders should not fall into the trap of commenting after every contribution because this stops free-flowing interaction. Members unwittingly can cause this to occur by posing questions of the leader instead of the group. When the leader prefers not to answer a question he can either return or redirect it. The *returned question* is the technique of turning a question back to the one who asked it in the first place. You can use this when you wish to help the questioner find the answer himself rather than provide him or the group with your version of the solution. This is a good approach when you want the group to solve the problem. There is a tendency for the group, especially if it includes your subordinates, to accept your solution rather than look for other alternatives. You should be watchful that returning the question is not overused. Of course, if you are asked for information as the logical source or the only one who has the data, it is inappropriate to return the question.

Consider the situation in which Tom has a problem in his department. As his practice is to depend too much on others to make his decisions, he has just asked you what you think he should do about the matter. During a meeting, you might turn the question back with something like, "Tom, you've brought up an interesting problem. On the other hand, you are nearer to it than anybody else and have lived with it longer than anyone here. I was wondering, on the basis of your experience, what you think might be the best way of handling it?" Notice this is not a "put down" but rather communicates an honest assessment of the situation as well as strengthening Tom's credibility. It should not be difficult for Tom to make some suggestions, and the group should be able to help him refine his ideas and support them.

The *redirected question* is similar to the returned question except that it is returned not to the asker but to another member of the group or to the group as a whole. You can do this when you know the questioner is not capable of providing his own answer. Suppose, in the example of Tom asking a question, you assess the situation and decide that he is not likely to come up with an effective answer since he has been in his position only a short time. Now your question might be worded, "Tom has brought up an important question. Can anyone help him out?"

Another method you might use is to direct the question to a group member who you know has had experience with similar situations. You might reply, "Tom has brought up a vital question. Al, didn't you run into this when you were manager of the night crew? How did you handle it then?" When asking this type of question, make sure that you are sensitive to the questioner's needs and avoid posing a threat to his ego or self-concept.

In addition to the types of questions already considered, you can use a variety of questions for other purposes. Too many leaders use the same pattern of inquiry over and over, regardless of the situation. How non-productive it is to find yourself in a situation where the leader uses only the returned or redirected question. So, for variety, keep the following kinds in mind.

1. A question which can be used to check understanding: "Your position is that we are overstaffed in certain departments but understaffed in others which results in some departments being overloaded. Is that it?"

2. To help the group understand the underlying reasons or to at least establish reasons for a policy or action, you might ask, "I realize that is the way we have always handled problems of this sort. I'm just wondering why we have dealt with them like that?"

3. You have just presented a plan which will affect the entire staff. You have worked hard on the proposed plan but realize that it may have weaknesses. You have just explained it to the group, and you want suggestions. An effective question would be: "I think this plan is basically sound, but I also realize it probably has flaws in it that I'm not aware of. Since this is important to all of us, have you any suggestions for making it better?" The secret to the effectiveness of this question is that you really want suggestions and you are open-minded enough not to become defensive or argumentative when the group amends or adds to your plan.

4. When the group is confronting a unique problem it might be helpful for members to explore their backgrounds for something that may shed some light on how to handle it. You might ask, "This certainly is a new one for us. We've been in business for a long time, and I don't recall ever running into anything similar to this. Do any of you have experience with this kind of problem?" Hopefully this will take the attention from the uniqueness of the problem and focus on the similarities with other situations.

5. If the group has been discussing a series of related problems but seems unable to make progress, the following comments might help: "We've been talking about several important problems. In fact, we've bounced back and forth from one to the other. Now, which do you feel is the core problem we should start with?" In this way the group is led to think about "which" problem rather than continuing to explore all the problems.

6. Let's say the discussion has been spirited but not very deep. To stimulate thinking you might ask, "We've been talking about a number of things, but maybe we're talking about symptoms rather than causes. What do you think are the real causes of our problems?" Notice that in questions like this you avoid bringing charges against any members, because, as a member of the group, you too may be just as much to blame. Also, we are not implying that the designated leader is the only one who can and should ask this question.

7. To arouse provocative discussion you may wish to act as a devil's advocate. The following questions serve this purpose: "This looks fine on paper, but have we anticipated all the difficulties we might get into if we establish the policy in one department and not in the others?" or "Do you think that a job-enrichment program would do anything for the people in that department?"

8. Another time to ask questions is when a new proposal has been thoroughly discussed; yet at times it seems the group is ready to implement it immediately while at other times you are not so sure. To determine the degree of reluctance or eagerness to move ahead, say something like, "There seems to be general agreement on the merits of the proposal. I am uncertain, however, where we are. Should we start as soon as possible or think it over until our next meeting before committing ourselves to action?"

9. You can also use questions to test for consensus. "We've looked at this from many angles and seem to agree on what we should do. Does everybody feel that this is the way we should go or are there some who have doubts?" A good leader makes sure that consensus has been reached rather than assuming that the vocal majority represents the feeling of all. Silence does not necessarily mean either consent or consensus. Be sure to allow enough time for response to this question. If you have established a non-threatening climate and have not committed yourself to a position, you make it much easier for those with doubts to speak up.

10. If the meeting has moved very rapidly, and the group has reached a solution very quickly—maybe too quickly—you might ask, "We all seem to be agreed about what should be done. But this represents a radical change, and I was wondering whether we're really comfortable with the decision. Would it be wise for all of us to mull it over for another week and then take it up again?" If this is a directive, don't try to disguise it as a question. If you want them to think it over, tell them. But if you only want them to consider it, then put it in the form of a question. If you use a question, be prepared to accept their answer.

You should be concerned not only with the extent and variety of questions that you have in your possession but also with your mastery of the art of asking the right question of the right person at the right time and in the right way. In addition to securing information, asking questions also serves to facilitate the interaction, to help others learn, and to build a spirit of cooperation among all the group's members.

Handling Problems of Participation

During the course of any group meeting, you are likely to face a number of irritating and awkward problems. One of these is the member who talks too much. Rarely is it appropriate just to cut him off; this may embarrass him and the others as well, and you may come across as being very authoritarian, if not dictatorial. Before deciding how to handle the over-talker, let's consider why he feels the need to hold the floor so long.

Really listening to him (fairly and without prejudice) often will help locate his need and give you a clue as to how to help him become effective in a group. Perhaps he needs recognition; perhaps he does not feel listened to or appreciated. You might want to meet with him outside the regular meetings and ask for his help with group problems such as assisting you in bringing out the shy, less talkative people.

Another strategy you might use if you have been unsuccessful with others is to ask a yes/no type of question of the talkative member during a meeting. Then, quickly follow the question with an open-ended query to another member. It might go something like this:

Leader: Just a minute, Keith, are you saying we should not adopt the new schedule?

Keith: Now, I didn't . . .

Leader: I just want to clear up this one point. You don't think we should adopt the new schedule?

Keith: Well, no, but . . .

Leader: Larry, I wonder how you see this situation?

This strategy should be used only after the member has had time to present his position and truly has become repetitious.

Another technique is the use of summaries. Two of the group leadership functions are summarizing and synthesizing the various contributions. If you interrupt a speaker to do this, it is rarely seen as a put-down. When you have completed your summary, simply direct a question to another member.

When all nondirective approaches have failed, as tactfully as possible simply direct the member to stop talking. You might try the following: "I need to stop you for a minute because that's an important point, and I'd like to get the reaction of some of the rest of us on that." Or, "Pardon me, but you have raised three or four points on this issue and before you discuss it further, I would like to spend more time on this one question of responsibility. What reactions do the rest of you have?" Or, "Can I ask you to stop there for a minute and hold your next comment? All the group has not yet had a chance to be heard on this point. I'd like to hear from them, and then we'll come back to you."

How best to handle the member who does not participate is equally perplexing. Almost every manual on conducting meetings stresses the importance of securing full participation from all members because groups need all their resources. The assumption is that if a member participates he will look more favorably upon the decision, be more inclined to feel that it is his own, and then do what is expected of him to implement it. Some of the current research has found, however, that the more important measure of members' satisfaction with a meeting is the extent to which they feel free to participate. It is important that when members feel they have something to say there are no barriers preventing them from participating. Your goal, then, is more realistic when you create a situation where everyone feels free to talk and not one where everyone *must* talk. Providing equal opportunity for participation rather than only equal participation is the key.

But how can we create such an environment? Once again, use of questions is your best approach. You may point out to the group that some have not had an opportunity to talk. Say something like, "Several of us have had a great deal of input on this matter, but there are some who have not had an opportunity to talk. Is there anyone else who wants to share his thinking on this matter?" The best kind of question is the open-ended one because if you ask a question that can be answered with a yes or no, you are likely to receive a one-word answer, leaving little to discuss.

If you use a direct question, be sure you ask one that the member can answer. Avoid putting the under-talker on the spot. This compounds your problem rather than solving it. A good approach is to ask for opinion or feeling, giving advance warning that you want to hear from everyone on this point. Start with the more vocal and move around to the less vocal last.

Handling arguments and resolving conflict may become problems for the leader. When handled properly, much value can come from these kinds of interactions. Actually, meetings need conflict and different opinions in order to fully explore ideas, solutions, and decisions. If everyone agreed, there would be no need for a discussion. When different views and opinions are presented, all have the responsibility to listen, to understand, and to interpret. It is only after this process that we should adapt, refute, or present our own point of view. It is the way we do this that matters. Try to help the group deal with ideas and not personalities. Such words as "opponents," "foolish," "uninformed," "shallow," or similar derogatory labels should never be used.

It also might be wise to avoid the use of the word "disagree" when you discuss the differences among the various ideas presented.

When you say, "Well, its apparent that Carl and Alice disagree on how we should handle this personnel problem," you may be intensifying their opposition, not resolving the problem. Instead of calling attention to the disagreements, point out the agreements.

It is from the area of agreements or common ground that you can help build new or bigger accords. In these situations, stress the logical dimensions rather than the emotional ones to avoid any personality prejudices. Don't be afraid of disagreements or arguments or try to gloss over them. "Pouring oil on troubled waters" may be a disservice to the group that needs to deal with its internal conflict. If the leader will focus on helping everyone understand each other's points of view, the conflict is more readily handled. Understanding and agreeing are not the same, but when people understand why they disagree they are much more likely to be productive.

A more difficult situation is finding yourself, as leader, in conflict and disagreement with one or all of the members of the group. If you are the person who signs the paychecks or has other sanctions over the group, you are hard to challenge; the others may not feel they can argue or disagree with you. Here are some suggestions on how you might respond to someone with whom you do not agree.

One of the best things you can do is listen—*really listen.* Your disagreement can block your hearing, but if you will hear the other person out, you may at least reach a level of understanding. While you listen, look for areas of agreement first. Avoid the temptation to focus on "where he is wrong." Make sure you understand to what extent you do agree with his point. There may be more agreement than it seemed at first glance. When you respond, restate his point clearly and fairly before continuing. Make sure you have stated it to his satisfaction, not to yours. Doing this sometimes can resolve the disagreement without further discussion because what we hear and what is meant are often very different.

When you do reply, try very hard to be pleasant. Watch your nonverbal message. Your facial expression, for example, may betray your irritation or displeasure. Try to be objective and to talk about the areas of difference with maturity. Make your position clear and support it with evidence and reasoning. In one sense you can never "win" an argument by destroying the other person's position or ego or by "pulling rank" to get your way. More is lost than won with these tactics. Your best bet is to try to conciliate or to find a compromise position. Above all, recognize the other's point of view from his standpoint (as well as his right to differ) before you begin stating and supporting your own position.

On Being a Participant

You will undoubtedly be a participant in a meeting more frequently than you are a leader, but it is a mistake to assume that only the leader has to know how to run the meeting. Every member should contribute to its actual running. As a participant, you should be just as alert to the way the discussion is or is not progressing toward its goals as when you are the leader. If the leader does not keep the meeting organized, allows the discussion to wander, fails to stimulate silent members, or otherwise neglects leadership functions, you may supply them. You must be careful and tactful in doing this, however. Don't compete with the leader or lie in wait for him to make a mistake and then leap to attention and point out his shortcomings. There is a good chance that the leader and the group will resent this one-upmanship behavior. Remember, too, that the other person's style of leadership may be different from yours, and your interference or intervention may hinder more than help.

Many of the principles discussed in this chapter are equally applicable to the group member as well as the leader. It is easy to take the participant responsibilities for granted, however, because attending a meeting looks like a simple thing to do. It may look so easy that you don't prepare but, instead, develop an attitude of indifference to the extent that you may attend in body only. You can be effective only if you take sufficient time and generate enough interest to prepare adequately for the subjects or issues to be discussed. It is an imposition on others for you to discuss an issue on which you are poorly informed. Pooling ignorance has never proved very useful. Preparation, then, involves both an attempt to find out all you can about the subjects to be discussed and the development of an attitude of wanting to participate.

Even deciding just how and when to participate is an important concern. Good participants have the ability to hold their tongues and listen while others speak. They listen for understanding and speak only when they have something worthwhile to say. If you sit back and say nothing until late in the meeting, you may find it hard to get involved or to get recognized when you want to contribute. Some studies show that those who speak early in the meeting have more over-all influence and gain more respect.

You should always be aware of the thread of the discussion and be ready to make your contribution. This sometimes requires split second timing, especially when someone is speaking who can filibuster at length on any subject. By listening carefully you may be able to start your remarks just as he or she is finishing, or ending a sentence. If you sit back and relax, the speaker may go on endlessly or some other member may break in and steer the discussion in another direction, and you may never get to make your contribution.

A good tip is to make sure your contribution, whenever you make it, is both relevant and related: relevant to the general topic and related to what has just been said. An effective technique is to "hook on" to the previous statement. Here are examples: "I think the point Dorothy made is a good one, and I'd like to add this . . .," and, "Along the lines of what George was saying. . . ."

There is no definitive answer, of course, as to how often or how much any member should participate. If we can avoid being either an over-talker or an under-talker, we are in good shape. We should be conscious of how much we are talking in relation to others. We should always avoid making speeches, even when we are tempted by the knowledge that we have the information or the experience that would most benefit the group. A good rule is to limit each contribution to one idea or one point.

As you participate in a meeting, apply all of your communicative ability to the situation. Perhaps the chief factor to keep in mind is the differences between people. Strive constantly to interpret the words, actions, and attitudes of other members in terms of *their* meanings and intents. This requires a constant "other-centered" attitude on your part as well as extremely alert listening.

All of us who have participated in, or led, business meetings recognize the need to make them better and more effective. To be sure, the leader needs special skills to handle his or her share of the responsibility, but the leader can be given valuable assistance by those attending. Skill in knowing how to participate in a meeting must be developed by everyone. When a positive attitude is substituted for a passive or negative one, greater accomplishments are sure to follow.

9
Decisions, Decisions

Stop a moment and recall the events of your day—or at least those of the last hour before you picked up this book. How many decisions did you make? Try to think of all of them, no matter how big or small, how personal or remote. Do you find this difficult? What have you identified as a decision?

You, of course, should not be surprised to learn that you are making decisions constantly. But when we asked one manager what was the biggest problem he had in running a business, he replied quickly. "It's all those decisions. That's all I do. It's making a decision about this, or solving a problem about that. It's like that all day. If it weren't for all those problems I'd have time to get my work done!" (We wondered how he separated his work from his problems, but we didn't ask.)

Decision-making and problem-solving are integral parts of the communication process. As communicators we are constantly involved in decision-making within ourselves or with those around us. Although

127

decisions have to be made in all interpersonal communication situations, the process itself is seldom something we think about consciously. Whether we are merely deciding when and what to talk about or who to elect as chairman of a committee, many decisions are made without our really being aware of how the decision was made or what effect it had on us.

A primary ability of the effective manager is to be able to make good decisions and to solve problems effectively. Too frequently these processes are regarded as natural; people are either born with the ability or they are not. But, as is true with most human behavior, including communication, such abilities are acquired and learned. Most of us have learned how to make decisions just by having to go ahead and make them and then live with the results. We watch how other people do it; then we plunge in, developing our own skill through trial and error. By now, the process is almost subconscious and done more by habit than design.

Some people are known for their snap decisions which they may come to regret later. Some people, on the other hand, seem incapable of deciding anything. They agonize over details and sway from one alternative to another, usually to the considerable annoyance of their associates. Still other people appear to be making snap decisions, but in reality they have quietly thought out the matter and have thoroughly prepared for the ten seconds in which it seems they spontaneously make their choice.

In this chapter we plan to discuss some of the principles of decision-making. We will offer a systematic approach to solving problems and show how these processes affect and are affected by our communication. These processes are learned behavior; they can be improved. We are always capable of learning to do them better.

It's More Than Apples and Oranges

Are decision-making and problem-solving really parts of the same process? What is the difference between the two? Can a problem be solved without a decision? Can a decision be made without solving a problem?

Actually, the processes are separate, but closely related, functions which at times overlap. Problem-solving has a larger scope and includes a wider range of types of behavior than does decision-making, but decision-making is no less important because of this. As a general rule we make many more decisions than we solve problems, but the two processes are inextricably bound together.

Look at it this way: During one day, a manager decides to (1) change a counter arrangement; (2) reorganize two displays; (3) take two employees off the floor to help him; (4) sketch out the plan; and (5) get suggestions from employees. In essence, the manager has had *to make decisions* and *communicate them* in order to solve his larger *problem* of "How can we improve our traffic flow?"

Thinking, Decision-Making, and Commitment

Whenever you walk through the business you are aware of various stimuli. You may be aware of various employees as they work, speak to a customer, inspect a new display. Generally, you are taking in all that is going on around you. You may be pleased or disturbed by what you see. This awareness, without any attempt to form conclusions, cannot be considered the kind of thinking which results in decision-making; certainly, there is no commitment. When thinking involves only a kind of kaleidoscopic assortment of ideas and associations and does not result in pulling them together, it cannot be regarded as thinking which will result in decision-making.

Decisions are the products of a thinking process which forms connections between ideas from which conclusions are drawn and to which we make a commitment. Decisions are made when we come to choice points or alternatives. Once made, a decision is the end of a process. (Often, of course, it is the beginning of still another process.) The decision-maker wants to achieve something; then he selects the alternative that will move him closer to his goal. What he really does, as he makes a decision, is to make a commitment or a personal resolution. Let's look at an example.

You have been sitting at your desk for well over an hour, working on one of those long, tedious reports. You are uncomfortable, and you decide it would be helpful to take a break, stand up, stretch, and walk around. You stop your work and carry out your decisions. The decision to perform the acts of standing up, stretching, and walking around is a commitment to perform certain behavior as a reaction to the discomfort of sitting and performing tedious work. Let's suppose you thought about taking a break, but then decided against doing so. Did you make a decision? Certainly. Deciding *not* to do something is just as much a decision as deciding to do something.

The significance of any decision is determined by the presence of a commitment. Commitment is not visible; only the behavior that results from a commitment is visible. We all have had the experience of having someone tell us they would do something, only to find it not done. Often the lack of action was due to the fact that the individual was not really committed in the first place. Phony agreements in which no real commitment is made have plagued mankind throughout history.

We must remember, however, that the process of reaching a commitment is not always rational. Much of it stems from our need system, our conditioning, our emotional makeup, and the circumstances that surround us at any given moment. It is easy to mix up the objective, impersonal aspects of the decision with feelings about its desirability or attractiveness or what other people will think or feel about it. The most logical, rational decision will be of no use if the emotional aspects are not weighed just as carefully as the facts. The decisions reached in the following example illustrate this influence.

A local manager is offered the district managership in another state. He discusses the offer with his wife, and they add up the pro's and con's. Logic tells them it is an excellent opportunity for the manager to move up in the hierarchy and make more money. Moreover, another offer may not come again soon or ever. Yet, emotionally, they are quite content in their present town and home and hate the idea of being uprooted. Will logic or emotion win? It could be either, but it is important to realize that emotions play as large a part in our decision-making as logic does. In fact, it is only logical to weigh our emotions along with the facts.

Although decision-making is not as complex a process as problem-solving, it does follow its own definite pattern. First, we become aware that we are at a "choice point" in which we must choose one behavior alternative from a group of such alternatives. Next, we examine the alternatives and predict the consequences of choosing each one. Last, we make our selection among the alternatives; in other words, we have made our decision. The second of these three steps is where we most often run into trouble because we are not always able to find out all we need to know about the alternatives and their potential consequences. Too often, we grab the first alternative that occurs to us.

Certainly we cannot solve problems without first making decisions. In fact, problems often arise *because* of decisions we make. Problem-solving is the organization of our decisions into a valuable and useful pattern. It enables us to cope with the conditions around us through an organized and rational system of related decisions and communications.

Some of the more familiar ways in which decisions are organized to solve problems are the following:

1. Let someone else do it.
2. Use an organized, rational procedure of studying and analyzing the problem.
3. "Sleep on it" until a solution occurs.
4. Wait for a sudden flash of insight that will reveal a solution.
5. Seek aid from another or bring a group together to work on the solution.

Regardless of the value of each of these approaches, decisions play an integral part in the total process. In problem-solving, the decisions are fitted together in a particular manner, as we shall now see.

Thinking and the Problem-Solving Process

Thinking and problem-solving are inseparable processes, because when we solve problems we have to engage in some rational thinking. Problem-solving thinking, however, has some special characteristics of its own.

First, problem-solving thinking has a purpose. It aims at a definite conclusion. It is not the sort of thinking you engage in as you are walking through a food store, and the particular smell of fresh pineapple reminds you of a vacation spent in Hawaii. Mental images form in your mind about the trip. In this kind of thinking, there is a connection or association between ideas, but your thinking is not aimed at any particular conclusion. Most social interactions, for example, involve thinking which forms connections in a loose, hop-and-skip fashion, but no one usually cares if a conclusion is reached or not.

Second, problem-solving thinking recognizes a discrepancy between need and capacity. Suppose you get into your car some morning to go to work, and when you turn the key in the ignition, nothing happens. The car refuses to respond, and your normal routine has suffered a jolt. What do you do? You decide that you either must get the car functioning again or find some other means of getting to work. Since you do not have time to call the garage to have someone sent out to work on the car, you check under the hood to see if you can spot the trouble. But your mechanical skills are not equal to the task. It is getting later, and you must be at work for an important meeting with one of the vice presidents from the district office.

The pressure builds. The bus has already gone by, you don't have time to call and wait for a taxi, and it is just too far to walk. What can you do? Suddenly you remember that some of your neighbors drive by your business on their way to work. You decide to walk to the intersection and hope a cooperative neighbor will drive by. One does, and you get a ride to work. Your immediate problem is solved, and the disequilibrium you experienced has been removed. Your long-range problem of getting the car fixed is temporarily postponed.

In this example, the problem-solving process was triggered by the discrepancy between what needed to be done (get to work) and your ability or inability to do that (finding transportation). Had your car started and functioned normally, you would have had no problem and, consequently, no need to do any problem-solving thinking.

What Is the Problem?

Sometimes, locating the problem *is* the problem. Many people, when confronted with the above situation, would decide that the problem is getting the car fixed. But that is really a solution to the principal problem of finding transportation. It is not as productive to work on the problem of how to build a better mousetrap as it is to consider how best to destroy mice.

It takes a certain amount of creativity to look for and correctly identify problems. Some managers feel they have enough problems already and wonder why anyone needs to go around looking for more. Other managers consistently ignore, evade, or escape tough problems that should be faced and solved. Still others seem to try perpetually to create problems where none exist. The competent manager tends to confront problems rather than evade them.

Characteristics of a Problem

As an effective problem-solver, you should be able to recognize the special characteristics of a problem. John Keltner isolates three elements of a problem which he calls the "goal-obstacle-encounter" triad.[1] All problems have these three aspects, he suggests. A problem does not exist unless there is a goal which is blocked by one or more apparent obstacles. As Keltner identifies it, the awareness of these obstacles is the "point of encounter." Below is a hypothetical situation that illustrates these characteristics.

You want to buy a new fishing rod (Goal). You are in a shop where rods are sold (Point of Encounter). However, you find that the rod you want costs more than the cash you have with you (Obstacle). In attempting to solve this problem, it is necessary for you to deal with all three characteristics. First, you might look at the goal. How strong is it? Do you really "need" the rod or would it just be "nice" to have? Would a less expensive one do as well? The degree of intensity of your desire to reach your goal will influence your attempts to solve the problem. Unless this desire is strong, you may just forget it, thus eliminating the problem. By changing your goal the problem ceases to exist.

The next element is the point of encounter. Let's suppose you did not enter this shop looking for a fishing rod but were shopping for other items when suddenly you saw the rod you would like to own. Now you are aware of your goal, and you have encountered the problem. You have no choice but to deal with the problem. (Remember, if you decide not to do anything, you have made a decision, too.)

Now that you know your goal, and you are not willing to change it or postpone it, you have encountered the problem and have run smack into the obstacle. How can you overcome the obstacle? Perhaps the store will take a check or credit card? On inquiry you learn that this is a "cash only" establishment. You realize that the solution to your problem may be more difficult to find.

This example illustrates how problems can be placed in this goal-obstacle-encounter format. Since these elements are so vital, a closer look is in order.

Goal

A goal is any condition which, if reached, will remove the effects of an undesirable situation. One day Fred, a department manager, stops you, his manager, to say, "You know those off-brand items we got in last month? Well, they're not moving. They're all going to go bad if we can't get rid of them. What should we do about it?"

---

1. John W. Keltner, *Interpersonal Speech-Communication*, p. 157.

The department manager has a goal: to sell the off-brand items. This could be your goal, too. Your objective might even be to help Fred be more independent in solving his problems. You could even have both as goals, but whatever you perceive as your goal will determine your response.

A goal may be simply one of escaping from a given situation. However, regardless of how we describe the goal, it must be regarded as a gain for the one seeking it, or he will be content to remain with the status quo. A good problem-solver will deal effectively with the process of goal selection. Some problems can even be solved right at this point.

Obstacle

An obstacle is any condition or object which prevents or hinders you from reaching your goal. If there is nothing blocking you, you have no problem. If nothing is standing in your way, your "problem" solves itself. However, in many problem-solving situations the obstacles are more imagined than real. The solution may be reached merely by realizing that what you thought were obstacles do not exist in reality. But, whether real or imagined, you cannot have a problem unless there are obstacles between you and your goal.

Encounter

Such elements as time, place, and circumstances bring you to an encounter with both your goals and the obstacles which prevent you from achieving them. Let's return to the illustration of Fred asking about the off-brand items. You encountered the problem when Fred asked what should be done. If you had no goals in this area, you would have no problem. This encounter makes you aware of your goals and the existence of obstacles blocking them. Your solution will be conditioned by your view of the situation, but the point is, you had no problem until you encountered it by interacting with Fred.

With a clear understanding of the goal-obstacle-encounter triad, further evaluation and integration are possible. You now have two courses of action open to you. First, you may try to find some way of overcoming or circumventing the obstacle in order to reach your goal. If you can find no way of getting around the obstacles, or if dealing with them is too expensive, involved, or time-consuming, you must change your goal. Of course, you may keep your goal and postpone resolution of the problem until you have sufficient re-sources or time. But in a sense this is still changing the goal since you have deferred the problem from an immediate to a long-range matter.

Suppose you have made plans to attend one of those intensive managerial training schools next summer. Everything is set; you have saved the necessary money, and the arrangement with your super-visor has been made. However, before you go, your wife informs you that your 12-year-old must have his teeth straightened. The ortho-dontist's charge will be well over a thousand dollars. You have a goal—going to managerial training school; you have an obstacle—the cost of the necessary dental work. You have encountered the situation through communication with your wife, and you realize the extent of your problem when you learn of the cost. You cast about for other means of resolving the problem, but it becomes clear that it is impossible to have the dental work done and go to the training program as well. You may decide to work for another year or two to pay for the dental work while you also save to pay for your training.

In this case you have changed your goal slightly by making it read "managerial school in two years" and have selected a course of action to achieve that goal. The steps you followed in this example constitute the structure of systematic problem-solving. But before we take a detailed look at this process, let's consider the role of goal-setting in the problem-solving procedure.

Goal-Setting

When you encounter a problem, the most critical step to take is that of goal-setting. Here is where communication plays a particularly important role. Although goal-setting may be done privately, we very often discuss and set goals with other people. This requires good communication skills, particularly speaking and listening. The views held by someone can be influential only if they are communicated and received properly. To set goals and solve problems together, we must constantly be alert to the factors which facilitate or inhibit communication.

The goals of your business may seem very clear: make money! But management goals are seldom that simple. While making a profit may well be an appropriate long-range goal, you must continually wrestle with short-range goals. Should your goal be production ef-ficiency and lower costs? Or should it be creating a mass demand or even a new "image"? Or all of them? If you are either uncertain of your goal or fail to see how it fits into the overall goals of the organization, you may find the quality of your problem-solving lacking.

When your personal goals are not in concert with those of the organization, difficulty can also arise. Many managers operate with a set of objectives which they believe to be compatible with those of the organization, only to learn that they have been in error. It is all too easy to assume that our goals are clear and mutually accepted by others. Another tendency is to assume that others rank these supposedly agreed-upon goals in the same order that we do. (Only good communication skills can remedy these problems.)

In one city commission goals became the rock on which the group actually broke apart. One faction of the commission contended that the group could not proceed with its work until goals were set so that the group would know where it was going and how. Another faction maintained that if the group plunged into a variety of activities, the goals would emerge and become evident. For a time the commission tried a compromise approach by spending some portion of each meeting on determining long-range goals and priorities. The widely varying perceptions and the ambiguous nature of the tasks, however, became too much for the group, and after one particularly bitter confrontation in which one faction accused the other of all talk and no action, and the other faction accused the first of "riding off in all directions without a horse," the chairperson and vice chairperson resigned. The rest of the group was disbanded by the city council.

There are at least two key questions that should be asked about a goal: Is it desirable? Is it attainable? The first is more important; if the goal is not one which would relieve the tensions you are experiencing, there is little point in asking the second question. You should answer the first question early in the problem-solving process; the second need not be answered until much later.

Too many desirable goals have been brushed aside because managers were either too lazy or not sufficiently ingenious to overcome the damning effect of those old assertions, "It can't be done" or "We tried it once, and it didn't work." We are all aware of so many things which are routine today, but which "couldn't" be done yesterday. It is far better to err by attempting the impossible than to reject the desirable.

By way of summary, here are five common reasons why goal-setting is often done poorly:

1. Goals are set too high or too low.
2. Goals are not properly agreed upon or adequately communicated.
3. Goals are accepted uncritically.
4. No real commitment is made to the stated goals.
5. Old goals are not updated.

Understanding the Forces

Another characteristic to consider is that most problem situations can be understood in terms of the forces which push toward improvement and the forces which resist improvement and keep the problem a problem. Sometimes the forces (thrust) are pushing for one kind of solution while opposing forces (counter-thrust) are pushing for another.

We must identify the thrust and counter-thrust forces affecting the problem and think about them broadly at first, then more specifically. Social pressures, physical resources, and personality differences are possible forces working for or against the status quo. A part of our problem-solving ought to be figuring out possible actions which reduce the effects of a force or eliminate it.

Figure 4

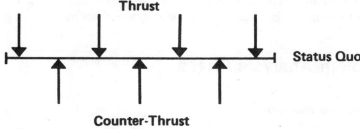

Thrust

Status Quo

Counter-Thrust

Systematic Problem-Solving

As we begin the examination of the problem-solving structure, don't be deceived by first appearances. Perhaps the sequence seems familiar, and you feel you know it already; but talking about the procedure and actually doing it have vastly different dimensions. We have worked with sincere and able men and women who could verbalize the necessary steps to effective problem-solving, yet were deficient when it came to applying the principles. It takes a degree of discipline to follow any procedure. If you have been accustomed to using an intuitive approach, this method may seem too rigid. On the other hand, not following such a sequence may result in such failures as lost profits, decreased motivation, and wasted hours.

It is impossible to solve problems without communication. At the very minimum, we communicate with ourselves about personal problems and potential solutions. More commonly, however, we need help from others to understand and solve the problem. We ask questions, make suggestions, and synthesize the written and oral expressions of many people. Everything about the communication process we have so far discussed in this book comes to bear on the systematic solving of problems.

Another important point must be made before we detail appropriate problem-solving steps. Although the steps logically belong in the sequence we will depict and we believe there is value in following this sequence, we recognize that flexibility is also important. In other words, the secret of successful use of the steps comes not from following them slavishly but in being aware of their existence and using them as a checklist or guide.

There are various methods of organizing the steps, but we have one which consists of two distinct phases—problem-solving and problem-solution.[2] Within each phase is a series of steps.

Problem Analysis Phase

Problem Formulation

In this initial stage you attempt to identify the elements of the problem confronting you. (Recall the earlier section of this chapter on the elements of a problem.) It may be that the goal needs to be changed or dropped. Whichever is desired, you should find out just what the nature of the obstacle is.

2. Adapted from the basic structure used in R.V. Harnack and T.B. Fest, *Group Discussion: Research and Theory* (New York: Appleton, Century, Crofts, 1964).

The life of a manager is filled with discrepancies. For example, there are discrepancies between what people tell you and what you know to be true, between what others believe and what you believe, between the things you want and your ability to pay for them—and any number of discrepancies between what is and what you wish it were. Perhaps no problems are more difficult to analyze and formulate than those which deal with employee performance. People fail to do things for many reasons, which, of course, leads to all sorts of other problems. But people problems come in many guises. Some are real and some are not. Spending time on solving a nonexistent problem is an exercise in futility. Since many managers find themselves doing just that, make sure you are solving what is a real problem.

You are probably in the presence of poor problem formulation when you hear any of the following statements:

"They're not doing that the way I told them."
"Employees just don't have the right attitude."
"Absenteeism is too high."
"I've got to teach our employees more about customer relations."
"We've got to train our workers to think more about safety."
"You've got to instruct your workers to be more profit-conscious."

In each of these statements the concern is with the proposed solution. Look over the statements again. Has the problem been clearly formulated in the mind of the speaker? You cannot expect effective problem-solving if the problem is unclear. The trouble with all the statements is that what has been identified as "the problem" isn't the problem at all. They are merely symptoms of the problem. Until the problem is understood in greater depth, proposing a solution is a hit-and-miss affair.

Problem Analysis

At this step, the goals and obstacles must be thoroughly examined, as well as the circumstances surrounding the situation. Most problems include a variety of goals and a variety of obstacles. By applying a rigorous analysis you can determine what the current situation is and just what must be solved.

During the 1960s many managers found a discomforting discrepancy between what they wanted and what they were getting with regard to the length of some young men's hair. Maybe you heard some of these managers say something like, "They should be ashamed of themselves. They can't work for me and look like girls." This translates into: "They must wear their hair the right way, like I wear my hair."

The discrepancy here is obvious: about three to six inches of hair! It was identified and even verbalized as such. But how important was it?

When one manager was asked about the significance of the hair problem, the following conversation took place:

"You don't much like the new length of men's hair, do you?"

"Is that ever true! It's disgusting and disgraceful. And we've got to stop it."

"It's clear you don't like it, but what would happen if you just ignored it?"

"What do you mean?"

"Well, just what would happen to business if you let it alone?"

"Well, it probably wouldn't make much difference to business. But they've got to have more respect for the company. They should want to look respectful instead of insulting."

Of course, the appearance of your staff (particularly those in direct contact with customers) is a communication in itself and unless properly managed, could be a barrier to achieving organizational goals. But today's managers have learned to live with many changes of hairstyle, as well as clothing and even life styles! Dress codes, once rigidly enforced, are now more related to safety and sanitation than to over-reaction to passing fads.

Not only must the discrepancy between the status quo and the goal be thoroughly investigated, but the goal and the obstacles must also be analyzed. Goals are seldom fixed; they are continually changing. When analyzing the situation, note where things are in relation to the goal and estimate where things will be if no significant change is made. As you examine the obstacles, be aware of their immediate effects; in addition, determine whether or not these effects will continue if nothing is done. Let us illustrate each of these.

In discussions of the problem of racial integration, disputes often arise between "liberals" and "conservatives." "Liberals" may insist that, unless aggressive measures are taken, there will be no perceptible improvement in the problem. "Conservatives" usually insist that the normal evolution of the status quo will eventually remove the problem without "revolutionary" changes.

If you are a parent, you are familiar with the numerous "phases" through which children are supposed to pass as they grow and mature. In the course of a child's development many obstacles to desirable behavior are discovered. The effective parent seeks to determine which obstacles will disappear in time, which need correction, and which need only modification in order to lay the foundation for appropriate development.

Finally, you should be aware of the changing nature of a goal. At first glance it may seem to be static since it probably was set by the organization. However, goals also must be considered as dynamic. This is true because of the changing obstacles and because of your own changing desires or needs. Consider the case of a couple deciding what kind of house to buy. As they face the decision, they must consider such things as family growth, changes in the city or neighborhood, and changes in the economic situation in general and for themselves in particular. In addition, they must also try to predict future changes in their own needs and desires. To some extent they can rely on others' experience in making these predictions, but the effectiveness of their decision is a function of how well they can anticipate these various changes.

Problem Reformulation (if Necessary)

If your analysis in steps one and two indicates a need to redefine the scope of the problem, this is the step during which it may be done. Actually, this step may occur at almost any point in the process. A good rule to follow is: do it whenever it is needed. When you begin your analysis of a situation you may have an idea about the nature of the problem, but as you dig further you may discover that the "real" problem is something else. Good problem solvers often reformulate their problems in light of their discoveries.

Several years ago an incident occurred in an automobile manufacturing company which illustrates this need. The company's problem was that it was running out of drying sheds in which to store its cars while the paint dried. A group of executives met to determine where and how to build more drying sheds. But land and buildings were expensive and construction was time-consuming. One person had a better idea: if the paint dried faster, more cars could be dried in the present sheds. The problem was reformulated. Instead of being, "How can we build more sheds?" It became, "How can we develop a faster drying paint?"

Criteria-Setting

Before you generate solutions to the problem, there is one last necessary step: identifying criteria or yardsticks by which the effectiveness of alternative solutions can be measured. Much time and wheel-spinning can be saved if the criteria are established *before* the solutions are proposed. For example, if your problem involves the selection of a new assistant manager, you would decide before you began your consideration what you needed and what qualities an individual should have to fill this position. These would be the criteria against which you would check all available applicants.

The selection of the criteria requires careful consideration. You do not need a perfect set of criteria because this prevents problem-solving. What is needed is a "satisfactory" set. Think of two people searching in a haystack for a needle to do a simple sewing job. There are a variety of needles in the haystack, and some are better than others. One person searching for the best needle, searches all through the haystack collecting all the needles he can find. He then measures the sharpness of each needle and selects the sharpest one.

By contrast, the second person who is looking only for a satisfactory needle, searches through the haystack until he finds a needle; then he tries it. If it is sharp enough to sew with, he gets on with his sewing, and that is the end of it. If it is not sharp enough, he keeps searching until he finds a needle that is satisfactory. Both people in this example have a set of criteria although one is more realistic for managerial decision-making. Some people use the search for the "perfect" solution as an excuse for procrastination and letting the problem go unsolved.

In the problem analysis phase, we have suggested that four steps are necessary. First, make sure the problem is clearly formulated; second, thoroughly analyze the problem; third, when necessary, reformulate the problem; and fourth, establish specific criteria. These steps are frequently slighted because as soon as a problem is mentioned, there is a tendency to begin suggesting possible solutions. It seems to be human nature to plunge into solutions even before we understand what the problem is all about.

Problem-Solution Phase

Solution Proposal

The problem-solving process is much broader than just selecting a solution. It must also include the search process for potential solutions. Research has proven that we would be wise not to settle for the first or second idea but instead to introduce as many possible solutions as we can that have any bearing on the problem. This isn't easy. The search may involve expenditures of time, energy, and even money. However, regardless of the cost, a problem cannot be solved adequately if we merely grab the first feasible solution that occurs to us.

The techniques of brainstorming can be very useful in locating possible solutions. This is a simple procedure that helps the problem solver avoid the pitfalls of bias and premature evaluation. The trick is to think up solutions in a free-wheeling atmosphere where no one is allowed to criticize or evaluate.

Here is how the process works. There is a specific, clear-cut problem with which you are familiar. First, see how many ideas for solving it you can think of. People who have used this procedure have found that the 33rd or 34th idea is sometimes more useful than the third or fourth one. Second, no idea is too wild. Let your imagination run free. It is easier to tame ideas down later than it is to create them in the first place. Whatever you do, don't be critical of your wild ideas because they just might trigger the one which will work.

Alex Osborn, the originator of this concept of creative problem-solving, provides an example of how this phenomenon occurred in one dramatic incident.[3] During the Korean War, a destroyer was becalmed in enemy waters and was in danger of being blown up by mines floating toward it. The ship was too close to shore to maneuver, making all usual techniques for dealing with mines useless. In desperation, the captain called on the men for any possible solutions to this potentially tragic situation. One sailor had the wild idea of having the crew line up on deck and try to blow the mines away from the ship. Ridiculous? Hardly. This "wild idea" sparked another idea that did work. Another sailor suggested that they use the ship's fire hoses to divert the mines around the ship.

Don't criticize ideas. Even a sarcastic smirk or giggle is out. As we have said, the evaluation of solutions should be a carefully separated step because it has been found that when the evaluation step is combined with the discovery step, creativity is limited. Be critical and analytic *after* all the solutions have been proposed. Some organizations even give the evaluation responsibility to a group separate from the idea-generators.

---

3. Alex F. Osborn, *Applied Imagination: Principles and Procedures of Creative Thinking* (New York: Scribner's, 1963).

The creative problem-solving or brainstorming technique has proved very effective in many situations. Business and industry have created better products, better packaging, and better solutions to all kinds of predicaments through this technique. One cautionary note: it is not the answer to all problems. The more complex the problem, the less likely this approach will be of assistance. The main benefit is the deferring of judgment until several creative solutions have been suggested.

It might be best to put the problem on the back burner and let it simmer in the subconscious. When faced with a knotty problem, it is wise not to attempt to work through the analysis and solution finding phases all in one sitting. Work your way through the problem description phase and then stop for awhile. You will find you are much more creative after you have given yourself a break. Many of the half-formed notions stimulated by the first encounter may be worked out in your mind when you get back to the problem again. Totally new and better ideas are usually the result.

Solution-Testing

A large part of the problem-solving process is, of course, the decision itself. After analyzing the problem, gathering all the information you can afford, and collecting as many alternatives as are efficient, what then? Decide on the best solution or a combination of solutions that appears to add up to the best without creating additional problems.

It is easy to assume that the right solution exists and that it will be selected, naturally. However, this is a questionable assumption. An equally dubious assumption is that people will select, rationally, the best solution from those laid before them. Two things are wrong with this reasoning. First, rarely will you have access to all possible solutions; second, you may have to be satisfied with something less than the "best" solution.

Action-Testing

A solution must be capable of being put into action, or it is actually no solution at all. The final steps in the problem-solving process are following through on the solution and putting it into action. We often reach general agreement about how to solve large or small problems, but later we find that nothing has been done. For example, you have discovered that your clothes do not fit properly due to an increase in your weight. Two alternatives seem appropriate: buy new clothes or lose weight. You have chosen to lose weight. However, this general solution to lose weight does not assure consistent rejection of desserts. A decision to increase your managerial skills by completing a home study program in management does not guarantee the act of studying day after day. Along with the selected solution should come decisions about who will carry out all aspects and how.

A further concern of the problem solver is the likelihood that solutions are seldom lasting. The whole problem-solving process should be regarded as a cycle rather than a one-way, one-time act. Some people are frustrated by the way problems keep cropping up. They wish problems could be settled once and for all. Life seldom accommodates that wish.

The Systematic Approach in Practice

Now that we have examined the steps of the problem-solving process, let's illustrate how one manager used them. Joe manages a large business which, like many other businesses, has a constant turnover of cashiers. For some time Joe has worried about the quality of the work his cashiers are doing and his continual problem of training new ones. He recognizes the significance of the cashier, who often is the only person with whom the customer has contact. Joe knows what the cashier says and does sets the image of not only his business but the whole chain.

Little by little, Joe's problem evolves in his mind. He eventually identifies it as "How best can we train our cashiers?"

Joe works first on *problem formulation* and determines that he has two *goals:* improved procedures and better work from the cashiers. He holds a meeting with his assistant managers, and together they work on *problem analysis.* They decide that the goals are viable ones. Solving the problem would improve efficiency, save money, prevent errors, please the customers, and improve employee morale.

Barriers to accomplishing these goals are the time lost from work by both the cashiers and those involved in training them and the work involved in planning and organizing a new training program. The managers report that they have tried to overcome these barriers by training new cashiers before working hours, so that the time lost will not be quite so expensive, and by doing an analysis of cashier efficiency in order to determine the most common errors or ineffective practices. These efforts have helped, the managers report to Joe, but more needs to be done. They decide that the consequences of letting the problem go unsolved will be lost money, lost customer goodwill, and a lowering of employee morale.

Joe and his assistant managers then move into *problem refor-mulation.* They look back at the two goals Joe had selected and they decide they constitute two separate problems. They agree to concentrate on better training of cashiers and treat the other goal of improving procedures as a separate problem to be dealt with later.

Now they are ready for *criteria-setting:* They decide it will be a good training program if: (1) new cashiers are faster, more efficient, more accurate, and better at customer public relations than untrained cashiers; (2) the cost does not exceed an agreed-upon amount per trainee; (3) the time involved does not exceed an agreed-upon number of hours per trainee; (4) the program can be smoothly integrated into existing personnel policies; and (5) the program will have some spin-off benefits to other employees who will also have training opportunities.

With their problem analysis phase completed, Joe and his team now move into the *problem-solution* phase. They hold a brainstorming session and come up with 24 ideas which they then evaluate, organize, and combine into the following six potential solutions: (1) expand on-the-job training by use of the buddy system, wherein an experienced employee works in tandem with the trainee for the first week or two; (2) hold orientation meetings for new employees on a regular, organized basis; (3) produce a regular publication covering "What every new employee needs to know" along with a question-and-answer column; (4) in cooperation with other managers in the division, organize a training school in a separate, central location; include a simulated business with fully equipped registers; (5) videotape cashiers at work and play back the tapes for evaluation and constructive suggestions; and (6) give awards for "Best Cashier of the Week."

Following solution proposals comes *solution-testing.* The group decides that number 4, the training school, is the best solution and that the next best would be a combination of numbers 1, 2, and 3. They rule out number 5 as too expensive and number 6 because it doesn't zero in on the problems of the new cashier.

For *action-testing* the managers decide to put one of the assistant managers in charge of working with representatives of the other businesses in the division to: (1) find an educational consultant to design a training program; (2) locate suitable space for the school; (3) build or remodel facilities; and (4) organize a training schedule in cooperation with the consultant. When they looked back at the criteria they had previously set, they were pleased to see that most of them had been met. Even the cost factor was within the boundary set because all businesses in the division would share in the expense.

The Systematic Approach to Problem-Solving

A systematic approach to problem-solving such as the one Joe and his team used is spelled out below. It can become an effective instrument with which to deal not only with managerial problems, but also with personal ones. Administrative staffs, organizations, work teams, committees, and individuals have all found such an approach useful in dealing with problems or with tasks that become problems.

Remember our earlier caution about not trying to follow the steps exactly and completely, however. Think of the procedure as a map that can help you get from here to there. Another use is as a checklist in case your usual problem-solving procedure doesn't seem to do the job. If you've worked to solve a problem and you are not satisfied with the solution, use this procedure to review what you have done and to discover what still needs doing. Maybe in the past you have been overlooking a step which could turn out to be the missing part of the puzzle.

In this chapter we have suggested that decision-making and problem-solving are different but overlapping processes. The process of solving a problem involves many kinds of decisions which are organized around central problems, goals, and communications. The systematic approach below is a process that can be easily learned and fully developed into an important managerial skill.

I Problem Analysis Phase

Step 1. Problem formulation
Problems are created by barriers which block goals. Problem-solving begins at the point of encounter. The process should begin with:
1. Determining the goal or goals sought
2. Identifying the scope of the problem
3. Excluding from consideration any aspect which is not relevant to the specific problem

Step 2. Problem analysis
In analyzing a problem, you must:

1. Explore the nature and worth of the goal
2. Discover and explore the barriers
3. Consider what has been done, or is being done, to overcome the barriers
4. Evaluate the effectiveness of these attempts
5. Determine the consequences if the problem goes unsolved

Step 3. Problem reformulation (if necessary)

After the analysis is completed, determine:

1. If the scope of the problem is the same
2. If the problem needs to be broadened, limited, or completely changed

Step 4. Criteria-setting

Before we generate solutions we need to identify the criteria or yardsticks by which their potential effectiveness can be measured. Some typical criteria for most problems are:

1. Cost factors
2. Time investments
3. Availability of resources

II Problem-Solution Phase

Step 1. Solution proposal

Proposed solutions are ways:

1. To remove barriers
2. To circumvent barriers
3. To make barriers ineffective
4. To supply missing or additional means of reaching the goal
5. To revise goals in light of barriers that are insurmountable

(All possible and satisfactory solutions should be considered)

Step 2. Solution-testing

Analyze the various solutions. Determine:

1. Their relative merit
2. Their potential effect upon the barriers and goals
3. Which solution or combination of solutions is the most desirable

Step 3. Action-testing

Putting the solution into action

10
Communicating Up, Down, and Across

Throughout this book we have contended that one of the greatest concerns any organization should have is with its communication. The modern organization is a complex structure of varied and specialized activities; it is only through communication that it is able to hold together and reach its goals. Effective managers must be able to understand the organizational as well as the personal interactions going on and be aware of the effects upon their subordinates and themselves. Before we discuss the role of communication in the organization, let's take a brief look at the nature of organizations.

What is an organization? There are many ways of answering this question but one good way to think of an organization is as an organic whole, consisting of interdependent parts with each having a special function or relationship to the whole. The entire enterprise is designed to transform the services of persons and things into a completed end product or series of end products. As individuals, we have limitations and weaknesses, but banded together through cooperative efforts, we are more effective than is possible through our individual efforts. Achieving cooperative goals requires communication, which is why we say that without communication an organization could not exist or function, and no real progress could be made.

Communication is vitally necessary throughout the organization. Through organizational channels flows the information that not only transmits orders and directions, but also achieves a community of understanding and cooperation, the division of work, the development of morale, the evaluation of performance, and the mobilization of the organization's resources.

Authority, to be effective, must be accepted by the subordinate as being consistent with his or her perception of the organization's goals. One of the major functions of management is to try to mesh the individual's goals as much as possible with those of the company; this can be done only through consistent and persuasive communication. An organizational communication system, therefore, supplements the system of authority. By understanding the communication system and using it effectively, we may strengthen the organization's structure.

In this chapter, we look at communication as it functions within the organizational system. We are concerned with the communication flow throughout the organization, barriers which impede this flow, and means the manager can employ to improve his or her role in this system.

Formal and Informal Systems

Some managers unwisely concern themselves with only the formal system of organizational communication, which is essentially message-processing following the lines of authority outlined by the organizational chart. Who is supposed to talk to whom is specifically delineated in the formal system. However, around the formal structure is an ever-changing and complicated network of informal communication channels that deserves attention as well. Employees know it as the grapevine; some managers disparagingly call it the rumor mill. This communication system is built not on who is supposed to talk to whom but rather on who actually does talk to whom, usually during coffee breaks and after work—certainly not at scheduled meetings.

We talked with one manager who planned to discuss a personnel change at her weekly staff meeting. The day before the meeting she realized that part of her staff were already discussing the impending change, and some of their "information from other sources" was inaccurate. Rather than let the grapevine produce more distorted messages, she quickly called the staff together for an impromptu session in order to give them the true story. This was smart management of both the formal and informal communication systems.

Directional Flow of Communication

There are three directions in which communication can be sent in an organization: up to superiors, down to subordinates, and across to colleagues on the same level. It is obvious that the bulk of communication in most organizations is downward—directing, instructing, explaining, and the like. The passing on of orders, policies, and plans is the backbone of managerial communication.

Although most communication in organizational networks is downward, we plan to spend less time with this aspect than with the less understood and often underutilized upward and lateral kinds of communication. Since the major emphasis throughout this book has been on the manager's communication with subordinates, we will take only a quick look at downward communication in this chapter.

Downward Flow of Communication

The greatest difficulty with most downward kinds of messages is their one-way nature. "Do as I say, not as I do!" the parent orders the child, leaving little opportunity for feedback, seemingly by design. Some managers also see communication as a one-way street, with only themselves controlling the direction.

We know of one manager who expressed this attitude when he said, "I'm responsible for making the plans, working out the schedules, and things like that. Then I give the orders to get all these things done. All my people have to do is carry out my orders. That's the only way you can run a business like this. Someone is responsible for giving orders and making decisions; someone else carries them out."

His attitude seems similar to the foreman who was having a lot of trouble with the union. Although he always seemed to be the target of union grievances, when he was contacted he invariably had the right answers. "You must have cooperation," he would insist. "Any time you have to enforce rules by force or discipline you've got trouble." But he continued to have his problems with unhappy employees. One day someone finally asked him what he meant by "cooperation." "What do I mean?" he echoed. "My people know what I mean. Do what I say and be quick about it. Now that's cooperation." With that definition and attitude it is no wonder he was a source of so many problems.

Those who share the views of the supervisors in the last two examples fail to see the values derived from encouraging employees to communicate fully about the policies and plans of the company. They are not likely to provide a clear channel for communicating information, opinions, and attitudes from their subordinates. There are many rewards, however, for the manager who is willing to listen and who urges subordinates to talk freely and honestly. We have already said that managers not only need to be receptive to upward communication from employees but also must actively seek it because upward communication is the chief source of that vital ingredient, feedback.

Upward Flow of Communication

A principal value of upward communication is that it is the means by which managers can discover whether subordinates understand their messages. We have pointed out elsewhere in this book that meanings are in people and not in the messages or words that we send to each other. It is through the process of feedback that meaning clarification occurs. If the channels are open—really open—then one can expect to eliminate many of the misunderstandings which occur all too frequently.

Through the upward flow of communication, the manager learns the degree to which his or her ideas are understood and accepted. In addition, upward communication helps create a spirit of cooperation which stimulates employees to participate in the operation of their unit. This also has the benefit of making them feel a part of the decisions, which in turn produces a higher degree of commitment. If there is good upward communication, management can receive valuable ideas for planning and improving the organization and its operation. Upward communication is not only the means of receiving "good" news; it also serves to alert the manager to problems which could, if not handled in time, develop into explosive situations which are definitely bad news.

It is one thing to talk about the advantages of upward communication but quite another to achieve it successfully. As we have emphasized, communication is dynamic and must flow up as well as down if it is to stimulate mutual understanding throughout the system. Communication has some of the characteristics of water which follows the path of least resistance, flowing down much more easily than up.

Take stock right now of the proportion of your communication that is upward; then divide that percentage into upward communication sought by your superior (in the form of reports or meetings, for example) and that which you initiate. This might provide you with a clue as to why you need to make more provisions to prime the pump and help your organizational communication flow uphill. If attitudes, feelings, and opinions are freely communicated upward, you can be warned of possible failure of your attempts to communicate. This may cause you to change your message or wait for a more suitable time to send it. It is through upward communication, then, that you know whether your downward messages have been understood, believed, accepted, or acted upon.

Gaining subordinates' acceptance of decisions is always a problem facing management. If there is free-flowing communication, if there is an atmosphere in which subordinates have the opportunity to participate in the decision-making process or at least to react and make suggestions about decisions, there is a greater possibility of acceptance and commitment. Understanding is not necessarily a product of receiving the facts, but is often the product of interaction in which the subordinate feels there is comprehension of his point of view. It is the feeling of being appreciated and "in the know," not the mere acceptance of ideas, that results in understanding and loyalty.

Upward communication is valuable not only to the manager but also quite important to his or her staff members, for it helps satisfy some basic human needs. Although most people see themselves as having inherent value and worth, when people do not have the opportunity to express their ideas their sense of personal worth is lessened. It is demeaning to be told what to do without being given the opportunity to reply, comment, or ask questions. This applies even if the communication is done well. It is a wise manager who not only allows but actually invites his or her subordinates to express their reactions to what they are told—and to do so before action is taken.

Since business organizations must be essentially authoritarian, it is especially important that every opportunity be given for subordinates to express their feelings to their managers. This is the place, within the unit or department, to counteract the frustrating impersonality a business organization often imposes.

We noted that it is much harder to make communication, like water, flow uphill than downhill. Let's talk now about some of the barriers which inhibit or block the flow of upward communication.

Blocks to Good Upward Communication

One of the main inhibitors to the free flow of information is inherent in the business organization itself. Often there is physical distance between people in the system. Top management personnel may be located in different offices, sometimes different cities, making access to subordinates a real problem. Another difficulty is time. The press of carrying out necessary duties is not often conducive to open communication; unless managers place a high value on communication, they are not likely to allow the time necessary for it to occur.

The rate at which a message can flow through the system can also be a barrier. Consider the following example. Doug has a problem in his department. It is one that must be considered at the top. He puts the message into the system by telling the manager about it. They discuss it for a couple of days; then, after reformulating it, the manager communicates it to the next person in the line of command.

It takes some time for that person to work on the case, gather some information, and think about it. Another three or four days pass. Finally, the problem is forward on to the divisional manager who keeps it on her desk for at least a week while she investigates and verifies the facts. After she is finished with her work on it, she sends it on to the vice president. And so on until the message reaches the top and then works its way back down. Weeks and maybe months have passed. What about Doug? Well, he left the company and is now working for a competitor. It's no wonder that many employees feel that it is hardly worth their time to try to communicate with management.

Not only did Doug's message take too long to work its way to the top, but it is very likely that as it passed through the various links in the communication chain it was diluted or distorted. Since each level of management consciously or unconsciously selects and edits the message, it becomes less accurate as it moves up. If the links are kept to a minimum, the message is more apt to remain reasonably accurate.

Not all barriers are caused by the nature of the business; some are put up by managers. If they seem anxious, impatient, annoyed, or distressed, their attitude will show and create a barrier against the flow of upward communication.

An innocent mistake on the part of the manager can seriously block communication. A business had been having a variety of personnel problems; morale was low. The divisional manager was brought in to talk with the employees to see if he could discover the problem. A meeting was held with the employees of one of the departments. The divisional manager, after giving much reassurance, was finally able to get them to talk. One of the concerns was with tardiness, not only in reporting to work, but also in returning from coffee breaks and lunch. One employee made the comment that since management did not observe these regulations on promptness, he didn't see why the rest of them should be expected to. Just as the employee made this observation, the divisional manager frowned and vigorously wrote a note to himself.

That did it. The employees interpreted the note as one which would be used against them. All the divisional manager had done was make a note to remind himself to talk with management about this practice, but the damage had been done. The employees were afraid to speak after that, and although the divisional manager made several attempts to resume the conversation, each failed and he shortly adjourned the meeting. One can argue that the employees ought not to have been so insecure or felt the way they did, but that doesn't change reality.

Is No News Good News?

It is easy to have the mistaken belief that the lack of upward communication means that all is well. One manager said, "If I've gone for several days without a complaint or criticism, I start investigating to find out what's wrong." He is not far off target. There is a great danger in assuming that one knows what subordinates think and feel. The professional manager makes sure that the communication lines are open.

Managers may find it unpleasant to listen to personal problems or discuss what appear to be trivial matters. To say to an employee, "Tell me about matters which are important but not about those that are unimportant," isn't much help. The employee's evaluation of the importance of a matter may vary greatly from yours. This resistance to listening may dampen the worker's willingness to communicate about anything. Also, personal problems and job problems are often closely linked, and it may be impossible to discuss each independently.

Whatever the topic, unless the employee finds a willing ear, communication is likely to dry up. As we have said, listening takes time and is hard work. Being pressed with all the daily problems and responsibilities makes effective listening doubly difficult. It is easy to turn an employee away with an apology for lack of time. However, many time-consuming problems could be minimized or eliminated if the manager were free to listen, for it is through listening that the manager can discover solutions to present problems or avoid future ones. Moreover, employees who can talk easily with their boss can quickly get the answers to their problems, which eventually may eliminate the problems or prevent them from growing into more serious ones.

The manager's philosophy of leadership is probably the most important factor in the flow of communication. If managers place high value on communication, they will free themselves to listen and talk with their people. They will spend time in developing their work force and in team building. On the other hand, managers who are aloof, who act unilaterally, who attempt to solve all problems by themselves, and who are unconcerned about the professional growth of their subordinates are apparently too busy to be concerned with communication. This type of manager seems to have a philosophy similar to that of a certain old frontiersman. While celebrating his 50th wedding anniversary, he was jokingly asked by one of his friends how he could live so long with one woman. His reply was serious. "Oh, it's not hard at all. She's the most wonderful person that . . . well, in fact, I love her so much it is all I can do to keep from telling her."

One manager complained to us that he was always the last one to learn about problems and criticized his employees for not keeping him informed. We asked, "How often do you discuss your plans and ideas with them?" "How often do you seek their advice and input while solving problems?" He admitted that he did this very infrequently. He believed it better to "keep his own counsel" until he was ready to act. This attitude does not generate upward communication, for to receive communication we must first be communicative.

Communication flows down through the organization much faster because management controls the lines and channels. It is not difficult for the manager to call a meeting of all the assistant managers. But how much more difficult, if not impossible, it is for an assistant manager to call a meeting of the managers. The subordinate does not have the same freedom to intrude upon the superior's time; neither does the subordinate have the facilities or receive the rewards for upward communication that are provided for downward messages. Many organizations have developed ways to speed and improve their efforts to communicate downward. Such aids as company publications or house organs, meetings, bulletin boards, and form letters are often available to management. Few such facilities for encouraging communication upward are available to hourly workers.

Messages from subordinate to superior cannot be prepared with as much care as those that move down. A divisional manager probably has a staff to help with communication, but this is not true of the salesperson on the floor. The superior should not refuse a message because it is poorly formulated or expressed in emotional terms. Managers who request all communication be put in writing forget that this may be a fairly easy task for top management, but it could be a real barrier to an employee.

Authority, power, and prestige are accepted dimensions of management. But the subordinate, who wants to communicate, must explain her- or himself and gain acceptance from one who has greater status and authority. Communicating from a position of weakness is always risky and difficult.

Bearers of bad news have rarely been rewarded. In fact there are historical incidents in which messengers who brought bad news were actually put to death. A remnant of this fear seems to persist in the business world today. Of course, there are those who seem to enjoy being messengers of gloom and bad tidings, but they are generally recognized for what they are. Unless superiors are particularly receptive, they can cause subordinates to withhold or downplay bad news, unfavorable opinions, and reports of mistakes or failures. It is only when managers are aware of these problems that they can respond effectively.

Facilitating Upward Communication

Some managers believe that all that is necessary to achieve upward communication is to be open-minded and receptive. Certainly this helps, but communication is much too fragile to overcome all the potential barriers with only open-mindedness. "My door is always open," is a good attitude to have, but it is hardly enough to ensure that people will walk through the door in sufficient numbers to produce adequate communication. Spontaneous communication is rarely balanced or comprehensive. You will hear about glaring weaknesses or outstanding successes. The aggressive and talkative persons from some departments may reach you, while individuals from other units remain quiet. The manager who depends on spontaneous communication alone rarely receives a true picture of conditions, nor the information needed. Upward communication should not be left to chance. Management must stimulate, encourage, and find innovative ways to facilitate its movement.

Upward communication is not like a radio that can be turned on and off at will. Attempts to improve upward communication must provide for its continuity. It is just as important to listen on difficult and overly busy days as it is when all is running smoothly. Managers who tune in and out to upward communication only when it is to their advantage or suits their convenience will soon find there is nothing to listen to.

There should be a clear, simple structure for upward communication. Too many subordinates don't know how to communicate up, and if they do, the channels or steps may seem so complicated they often decide to forget it. Meetings and interviews, which were discussed earlier, are effective means of producing upward communication. Subordinates need to know when, to whom, and under what circumstances, they should talk. There are advantages to having messages "go through channels" but not if the structure is so cumbersome it becomes a barrier. Communication should be allowed to flow upward until it reaches that person who is responsible for, or who can take action upon, the problem or situation communicated.

Upward communication requires sensitive reception and the realization that people see the world differently. The way the divisional manager sees the organization is vastly different from the way the part-time employee does. We all see and interpret things according to our meanings and values. Managers who expect employees to look upon the importance of efficiency, safety, profit, and such matters exactly as they do are bound to be disappointed. Communicating with employees, trying sincerely to get their interpretations and ideas, is absolutely essential. Managers make a serious mistake when they assume that a certain set of facts will lead to the same conclusion in the subordinate's mind as it does in their mind.

We have already discussed the reluctance of some subordinates to pass on unpleasant information. They are naturally concerned whether it will offend or annoy, whether they will be regarded as disloyal for listening to criticism or for passing it on, and whether their boss is secure enough to hear unpleasant news. The wise manager is constantly alert to his own behavior in such interactions. He carefully listens to the tone and rate of his own speech. He knows that subordinates are especially alert to nonverbal actions, such as movements of the head and body, grimaces, silences, smiles, and scowls, the drumming of fingers or the clicking of a ballpoint pen lever. The setting of the jaw or the reddening of the face may say, "Stop, I don't want to hear anymore!"

Upward communication is rarely effective if the subordinate sees it as "upward." Who wants to talk "up" to anyone? Effective managers must rid themselves of feelings of great superiority and be extremely careful that their manner does not imply that they are either condescending or patronizing.

Although the following story takes place on a beach and not in a business, it has a colorful and telling way of illustrating almost all we have been saying about upward communication.

"The Fable of the Ill-Informed Walrus"

(Originally printed in the *Newsletter* of the Association of Management in Public Health, April, 1962.)

"How's it going down there?" barked the big walrus from his perch on the highest rock near the shore. He waited for the good word.

Down below, the smaller walruses conferred hastily among themselves. Things were not going well at all, but none of them wanted to break the news to the Old Man. He was the biggest and wisest walrus in the herd, and he knew his business—but he did hate to hear bad news. And he had such a terrible temper that every walrus in the herd was terrified of his ferocious bark.

"What will we tell him?" whispered Basil, the second-ranking walrus. He well remembered how the Old Man had raved and ranted at him the last time the herd caught less than its quota of herring, and he had no desire to go through that experience again. Nevertheless, the walruses had noticed for several weeks that the water level in the nearby Arctic bay had been falling constantly, and it had become necessary to travel much farther to catch the dwindling supply of herring. Someone should tell the Old Man; he would probably know what to do. But who? And how?

Finally, Basil spoke up. "Things are going pretty well, Chief," he said. The thought of the receding waterline made his heart feel heavy, but he went on: "As a matter of fact, the beach seems to be getting larger."

The Old Man grunted. "Fine, fine," he said. "That will give us a bit more elbow room." He closed his eyes and continued basking in the sun.

The next day brought more trouble. A new herd of walruses moved in down the beach, and with the supply of herring dwindling, this invasion could be dangerous. No one wanted to tell the Old Man, though only he could take the steps necessary to meet this new competition.

Reluctantly, Basil approached the big walrus, who was still sunning himself on the large rock. After some small talk, he said, "Oh, by the way, Chief, a new herd of walruses seems to have moved into our territory." The Old Man's eyes snapped open, and he filled his great lungs in preparation for a mighty bellow. But Basil added quickly, "Of course, we don't anticipate any trouble. They don't look like herring-eaters to me—more likely interested in minnows. And as you know, we don't bother with minnows ourselves."

The Old Man let out the air with a long sigh. "Good, good," he said, "No point in our getting excited over nothing, then, is there?"

Things didn't get any better in the weeks that followed. One day, peering down from the large rock, the Old Man noticed that part of his herd seemed to be missing. Summoning Basil, he grunted peevishly, "What's going on, Basil? Where is everybody?"

Poor Basil didn't have the courage to tell the Old Man that many of the younger walruses were leaving every day to join the new herd. Clearing his throat nervously, he said, "Well, Chief, we've been tightening things up a bit. You know, getting rid of some of the dead wood. After all, a herd is only as good as the walruses in it."

"Run a tight ship, I always say," the Old Man grunted. "Glad to hear that everything's going so well."

Before long, everyone but Basil had left to join the new herd, and Basil realized that the time had come to tell the Old Man the facts. Terrified but determined, he flopped up to the large rock.

"Chief," he said, "I have bad news. The rest of the herd has left you."

The old walrus was so astonished that he couldn't even work up a good bellow. "Left me?" he cried. "All of them? But why? How could this happen?"

Basil didn't have the heart to tell him, so he merely shrugged helplessly.

"I can't understand it," the old walrus said. "And just when everything was going so well!"

Obviously, managers should avoid selecting only those subordinates from whom they wish to hear. Selectively listening to those whose ideas are similar to ours may give us a pleasant picture that all is going well; but all will be well only in our fantasies. The "yes man" has never been known for his ability to reflect or report reality. Line men must listen to staff assistants, top managers to junior executives, managers to department heads, union stewards to foremen, and vice versa, with the same interest and respect that they expect themselves.

Simply receiving a message often implies to the sender that action will be taken. However, just letting a person vent his or her feelings does not always dissipate the problem. When the complaint concerns an ineffective or outdated policy, listening without taking corrective action is not much help. Managers who think they can listen sympathetically to justifiable complaints and, by this, satisfy the needs of subordinates are fooling themselves.

Nondirective counseling has value in helping an employee solve his or her own personal problems, but it has almost no value in helping to solve problems which are outside the individual. When receiving a communication, wise managers will not appear to agree with it unless, of course, they do. They do not indicate that corrective action will be taken unless they really plan to do so. If nothing can be done, or should be done, they explain why in order not to mislead the employee to expect changes or improvement. When led to expect action and none is forthcoming, the employee is properly resentful. If good suggestions are not used, or if they are put into effect without the employee receiving credit, upward communication tends to dry up.

In summary, upward communication serves a vital need of the manager. Free and open communication with the work force fosters growth of democratic leadership, satisfies the need for participation and expression, and promotes loyalty and respect for the company. It provides the manager with a clearer picture of the dynamics of the organization, helps in locating problem individuals or situations, taps new ideas and solutions, and increases the possibility that downward communication will be both understood and acted upon.

The Upward Communication of the Manager

In the previous section we talked about how managers could remove the barriers to upward communication which might interfere with the flow of communication from their subordinates. But the flow should not stop with the manager. As a manager, you also are responsible for communicating with your superiors. In this section we discuss the manager's role as upward communicator.

One rule that the competent manager learns is: "Never let the boss be surprised." This is accomplished through full and open communication. Your supervisor should hear first from you about any unusual success, unusual circumstances, and, of course, about your occasional failures. Your relationship will not be enhanced or your credibility increased if your boss stumbles into your mistakes or hears about them through the grapevine. Your success, or lack of it, depends to a great extent on how well you keep your boss informed.

Managers who are effective at upward communication have mastered three fundamentals: they know the duties and responsibilities of their position; they understand the needs of their superiors; and they understand their superiors. Ineffective managers may see no need for telling their superiors anything or, at the other extreme, may try to be a substitute for the daily newspaper. It is not the responsibility of managers to keep superiors informed on world events or general economic conditions. Nor should they waste time passing on idle rumors. Good managers can tell the difference between gossip and genuine concerns.

Managers cannot hope to be effective communicators with their superiors unless they have a clear picture of their responsibilities. When we asked one manager of a big department in a discount store about his responsibilities, he laughed and said, "Well, that's a big one. There are so many and they are always changing. Basically, I do what has to be done." "Do you think you're meeting the expectations of your boss?" we asked. "As far as I know, but that's a problem. There are always so many changes, new people, and all. I never know for sure just what authority I have. About all I can do is hope for the best." We left with the feeling that he did not have a clear understanding of either his authority or his responsibilities.

Of course, in this example it did not seem that all this uncertainty was his fault. But regardless of who was to blame, he would probably have a difficult job communicating effectively with his superiors. Managers who do not have a clear understanding of what is required of them should seek an early discussion with their supervisors to clarify their duties and responsibilities. It is impossible to communicate effectively about our responsibilities if we don't know what they are.

Delegation of Authority

Your position implies that you have been delegated certain authority and responsibility. For you to be effective you must also understand the extent of this delegation. Some duties are delegated completely, and you may have the entire responsibility for carrying them out. When this is the case you may have the authority and responsibility to make decisions without necessarily having to report them to your superior. But not everything is delegated completely. The manager who assumes this is the case may fail to meet the communication expectation of his or her superior.

Typically, most managers find their work falls in this second category of partial delegation in which they have the right and freedom to make decisions but they are also expected to report upward later. Routine actions need not be reported daily but should be included in regular, periodic reports. On the other hand, an action of an exceptional nature and which may affect the entire organization, or your superior, should be communicated to the superior directly and immediately.

A common error is to assume that delegation of authority and responsibility means that the authority and responsibility have been shifted from one person to another. If the manager thinks that what has been delegated to him are now his problems and are no longer any concern to his superior, he will not likely report effectively on his activities, if he does so at all. Such a manager is headed for trouble. Similarly, if a manager feels the matters which he delegates to his subordinates are now their problems and no longer concern him, he is also headed for trouble. No one can wash his hands of a problem by delegating it, and it is only through free and unrestricted communication that managers stay in contact with all of their responsibilities, delegated or not.

"Why is communication important? I'll tell you why. That's how I find out the decisions I've made," said a vice president. It was said in jest, but he was more than semi-serious. His subordinates' decisions became his own decisions.

No matter how delegation occurs, everyone is still responsible or accountable for what has been delegated to him even though he, in turn, has delegated it to another. When the manager fully understands the function and nature of delegation, he realizes why his superior needs to know what decisions he has made. Your superior is not being nosey or idly curious when he requests reports about your activities. In most cases, he must report to his own superior about the decisions he has made, which of course, include those you have made.

Understanding Your Superior

In addition to understanding the duties and responsibilities of your job and the nature of delegation, it is also vitally important to understand your superior as an individual. This knowledge may affect the form and frequency of your reports. Maybe your superior is the kind of person who likes charts and graphs with a lot of statistics; try to meet these expectations. But if he or she dislikes this form of reporting, adjust. This may seem very obvious, but we have had people from upper levels of management complain that they wished their people knew how to make or write better reports and we wondered if they had ever told their subordinates what was expected of them.

When does your superior like to hear from you? When does he expect your reports? The manager who knows the answers to these questions and responds appropriately is more likely to be heard. Try to avoid surprising your superior with a disturbing communique just before he leaves for an important business trip or on his vacation. Common sense dictates that only the most urgent matters should be brought up at such a time.

Selecting the appropriate information, problems, accomplishments, and failures to communicate upward is never easy. Most organizations and businesses have established reporting forms which provide clues to the routine information needed. In general, superiors need information in four basic categories: (1) status of long-term projects; (2) completion of specific task assignments; (3) deviations from the established operational procedures; and (4) forecasts of any anticipated problems. Let's look at each of these a little more closely.

In addition to your regular duties, there are probably assignments to work on special projects which may be continuing or long-term. Your superior needs to be kept informed as progress is made, but you will have to decide the format and frequency of such progress reports. These should not be hit and miss. Find out what your superior wants and when.

Reports on the completion of special assignments are always desirable. Most of us have learned through sad experience the fallacy of assuming that a job has been done because someone was told to do it. Have you ever had a complaint from a subordinate that he had not received recognition or praise for completion of an assignment? The reason may have been that you were unaware that the assignment had been completed. If the employee fails to inform you, it is difficult to make an appropriate or timely response. The same situation is true, of course, in passing along information to your own superior.

The reports on progress being made and the completion of tasks are usually good news and are pleasant to report. But if, suddenly, you are aware that it is necessary to deviate from the regular procedure, perhaps because of illness of key employees, a delay in receiving merchandise, severe weather conditions, or a breakdown in equipment, the news may not be so pleasant to pass along or receive. In a situation of this kind you must take action, but as soon as possible or appropriate, you need to report both the problem and the solution you decided upon to your superior.

Any deviation in approved procedure may require additional changes in other procedures. The quicker this is known by your superior the better he is able to respond and prevent the problem from snowballing. His experience may provide you with ways of coping with the situation, and he may suggest alternative courses of action. Perhaps he can authorize other changes which will help to deal with this deviation. All of this requires open communication.

Another type of deviation which should be communicated quickly is failure. Mistakes or failures should be reported immediately to minimize any serious effects. A mistake is easier to overlook if it is not made often and is reported promptly. If you ignore or gloss over mistakes and they are found out later (as they usually are), your boss has two legitimate criticisms. He can hold you accountable first for making the mistake, and, second, for trying to conceal it. It is never easy to admit an error, but it is less painful than being doubly reprimanded.

Predictions of future problems and situations also take the form of reports to your superior. Although your job description probably does not include this point specifically, it surely implies that you have the responsibility and authority to make recommendations on any subject which affects the well-being and future of the business. The successful businessperson always must be thinking of the future. Reports of what has happened are vital, but predictions of what will happen can be even more important. The major interest of a business is not how much money it made last year, but how much it can expect to make next year. The competent executive is the one who anticipates the problems which are ahead and is able to make viable suggestions toward their solutions. Solving today's problems is of first concern, but had they been anticipated they might not have become problems.

You can keep your boss informed through either oral or written messages, but which is better? There is no right answer. Some should be written, others spoken, depending on such factors as complexity of the message, urgency, and the number of people who should receive it. Another aspect to be considered is the message receiver. Regardless of relative intelligence or ability, two people may vary greatly in their tendency to respond best to either the oral or written word. We usually find out by trial and error which method works best for which person.

Written Upward Communication

In general, there seems to be too much dependence on the written message for most organizational communication. The following situation illustrates this.

Because of a misunderstanding of an oral instruction which cost the company a severe loss, top management met and came up with the directive that "all important messages will henceforth be put in writing." They also selected a slogan, "Write it! Don't say it!" which was printed on all their publications, memos, and letters. Signs were made and placed throughout the various branch locations of the organization. Everywhere an employee looked, the slogan looked back at him.

One day a new manager was preparing a report which he asked his secretary to type.

"How many copies do you want?" she asked.

He wasn't prepared for this. No one had told him he could have more than one copy. But he was equal to the occasion, for he came back with a sly question. "How many copies can I have?"

"Oh I can make five good carbons, maybe six," was the response.

"Make six copies, please," said the manager because he had just had a brilliant idea. Why not send copies to the other managers to let them know what he was doing? In time, the copies were distributed and the idea caught on. Other managers began sharing everything they wrote, every idea they had, and sometimes even memoranda they received from others. Soon the company bought additional duplicating equipment, and the situation escalated. A flood of paper descended on management until it became necessary to employ new people to read and file it.

Oral Upward Communication

The above may sound like a fable, but have you looked at all those papers on your desk lately? What about those files full of reports? Don't forget those you take home to read after dinner. Is it safe to say that you are drowning in a sea of paper?

This does not suggest that written communications should be abandoned or that oral reports are always best. An oral report has apparent advantages in not seeming to require much time for either preparation or transmission. But an effective oral report is really quite carefully prepared and not blurted out "off the top of your head." If it isn't prepared it may require considerable interaction to bring out all the facts and end up taking more time than it might have saved. One of the real advantages of the oral report is the opportunity for two-way communication between you and your boss. One of its disadvantages is that there may be poor records kept of those items which should be preserved.

On many important matters there should be both a written and an oral report. After a discussion with a superior, it is often valuable to follow it with a written summary of your understanding of what was discussed and decided. This memorandum can be referred to higher levels in the company, when it is desirable to do so. If you submit a report before a scheduled meeting with your superior, it may give him the opportunity to prepare more effectively for the meeting.

If you want to keep your boss informed and help him make decisions, be certain that he receives all the necessary facts. However, if you don't have all the facts, admit it. Moreover, be careful to distinguish between facts and inferences. Facts can be seen or observed. Inferences are interpretations which are concerned with degrees of probability. Believing in something does not make it a fact, but it is easy to yield to this tendency.

When you are reporting on a problem, try to have some possible suggestions as to what might be done. You have almost unlimited authority and responsibility to make suggestions and recommendations. Use it. But when you make your recommendations, be prepared to accept someone else's solution or plan. It is even advisable to have alternative approaches to the problem. Remember that there are very few problems, especially where people are involved, that can be solved in only one way.

Communication With Peers

Your job is to get things done through people. Sure, you've heard that before. But when you think of it, usually the people referred to are your subordinates, and sometimes, your superiors. Too little attention, we feel, is given to the importance of effective communication with peers. Do you have any responsibilities to your equals in the organization? Does this relationship have any effect on the operation of the various units or departments? Let's turn our attention to communicating across or laterally.

We have already talked about the necessity for maintaining a cooperative relationship throughout an organization if the company is to reach its goals. You are more likely to get cooperation from your peers if they know what to expect from you. For example, are you consistently on time? What about meeting deadlines for reports? Can the personnel director count on receiving your merit ratings on schedule? All these functions and the way you handle them communicate something to your peers and affect the degree of cooperation you can expect.

In one business, it was customary for employees to get their paychecks from the main office. However, one department manager started picking up all the checks for his people and passing them out in his department. He thought it added a personal touch and gave him an opportunity to express appreciation. But this unilateral action caused friction among the other employees and resentment from his peers. Finally the manager had to call a special meeting to resolve the conflict. This unit manager made the mistake of assuming that his decision would affect only his department.

Each manager should check out such decisions with others to make sure they will not put other people on the spot. A narrow perspective can be damaging when you are trying to promote an idea that you think will help your team. There is nothing wrong in being loyal to your group, but you should not forget that you are only part of a larger enterprise.

Going to the other extreme can be just as dangerous. Being willing to give in all the time can be bad for your team as well as for the company. Companies develop and grow because of innovations. Fight for ideas you think are good and sound. Be ready to meet objections with reasoning and logic. Show how your ideas will benefit other departments as well as your own. But there comes a time when compromise is necessary and the best solution or policy is chosen because it meets the needs of all the people, not just those on your team.

One manager appointed five assistant managers to serve as a committee to plan the annual picnic. At the first meeting, four of them had excuses why they could not help and left the picnic for the chairperson to arrange. The picnic was a flop, and the chairperson was blamed; but the fault really lay with the other managers who had failed to assume their share of the assignment.

A sure way to create hostility and block communication is to renege on your part of a bargain or policy. For example, one group of managers agreed that they would not give Christmas gifts as they had done in the past. But one manager gave in at the last minute and bought gifts for his staff anyway. As a result, the rest of the managers were made to look cheap. Of course, the offending manager had real difficulty restoring communication and a spirit of cooperation with his peers after that episode.

There are times when a manager has a perfectly valid reason for not meeting an agreed-upon deadline or following an agreed-to plan. Don't be too quick to criticize or blame. You may find that emergencies or unexpected difficulties have required the change. However, the manager who has to deviate from an agreed-to plan has the responsibility of communicating this to the other managers.

Is it possible to disagree with your peers without making them angry or turning them into enemies? Yes, if you are careful to follow some suggestions. First, don't become angry yourself. When you disagree, do so in a reasonable manner. Avoid such statements as, "Where in the world did you get an idea like that?" It is unrealistic to expect a logical argument from someone who has just had his intelligence questioned.

When you disagree with a peer, express yourself in straightforward, simple, and unemotional words. Disagree with ideas, not with people. Communicate "I may dislike your idea, but I like you." If you can separate the idea from the person, you may be surprised how often suggestions are accepted, or at least listened to.

For example, you've turned in a report to your boss who says to you, "This is a lousy report." Certainly not good to hear and not very good supervision. But suppose the boss had said instead, "You are incompetent." Most people would agree that this is worse. Why? Because the first statement is directed at the report; it is within your power to change it and improve upon it. But the second is directed at you, and, seemingly, there is nothing you can do to "become competent." This, therefore, is a personal putdown aimed at the person, not the report.

In this chapter we have been concerned with the important role communication plays in the operation and function of the total organization. Communication is the organization in action. It is the way in which the parts interact and affect the whole. With the increasing size and complexity of the modern organization, great strain is put on the system of communication which is needed to keep the organization together and functioning.

No matter how many devices are developed as transmitters of information, the real test of cohesion and cooperation will be the ability of human beings to understand the meaning of messages, their willingness to share ideas, and their respect for their colleagues. Communication is everyone's responsibility. Its flow through an organization is only as effective as its flow among the individuals who make up that organization.

Index